DICTIONARY OF CHINESE CLASSIFIERS

汉语量词词典

汉英对照
With English Equivalents

王达金 · 吴志芳 编著

平安国际出版社
HEIAN INTERNATIONAL, INC

© 1989 Federal Publications (S) Pte Ltd

First American Edition 1989

HEIAN INTERNATIONAL, INC.
P.O. Box 1013
UNION CITY, CA 94587

ISBN: 0-89346-312-4

Printed in Singapore

前　言

　　汉、英两种语言在量词表达方面是不同的。有的英文表达方式比汉语复杂。比如：a group of children, a gaggle of geese, a flock of sheep, a herd of cows 等几十种表达形式，都可用同一个汉语量词"群"。然而，更多的英文表达方式要比汉语简单得多。比如：a horse, a cow, a bird 等，在汉语中根据不同对象，必须采用三个不同的汉语量词。a horse 指一**匹**马；a cow 指一**头**牛；a bird 指一**只**鸟。

　　此外，有些汉语量词虽然不同，但意义相同。比如："一群人"和"一伙人"中的"群"和"伙"意义相同，都可用 a group of people 表示。又如：a building 指"一栋楼房"或"一幢楼房"，其中的"栋"和"幢"意义完全相同。

　　正因为汉、英两种语言在量词表达方面的极大差别，不仅给每一个英文学习者，而且给每一个汉语学习者带来了不少困难。为了帮助读者正确理解和运用汉语量词以及相应的英文表达方式，我们编写了这本书。

　　这是一本专门研究汉语量词以及相应的英文用法的书。本书收集了汉语中所有的量词及其英文表达形式。每个量词都配有适当例句，进一步帮助读者理解和运用。

本书目录按汉语量词的汉语拼音的字母次序排列。书末附有英文名词与汉语量词对应索引表，按英文字母顺序排列，便于使用时查阅。

在编写过程中，我们参阅了中外有关工具书，为避免累赘，恕不一一注明。本书初稿承蒙华中师范大学英文系主任李华矩教授认真审阅，提出了不少宝贵意见；邓祚智、蔡荣春二位先生对本书的编排及有关内容提出了不少宝贵的意见，并作了具体修改；在此，我们谨表谢意。

编者

1988年1月

音序目录

把 bǎ

①指一只手抓起的数量；　②有把手器具；
③指手的动作次数；④用于某些抽象事物。

一把······a bunch of; a bundle of; a handful of; a pair of.

一把花　a bunch of flowers
Peter gave Mary a bunch of flowers when he came to see her.
彼得来看玛丽时，送给了她一把花。

一把筷子　a bundle of chopsticks
Please buy a bundle of chopsticks on your way back.
请你回来时买一把筷子。

一把米　a handful of rice
Don't forget to feed the chickens with a handful of rice every morning.
别忘了每天早晨喂小鸡一把米。

一把种子　a handful of seeds
He sowed a handful of seeds in the field.
他在这块田里播了一把种子。

一把泥土　a handful of soil
He brought us a handful of soil from our hometown.
他给我们带来了一把故乡的泥土。

一把糖果　a handful of candies (sweets)
She gave a handful of candies to each of us.
她给我们每人一把糖果。

一把瓜子（花生）   a handful of melon seeds (groundnuts)

Have a handful of melon seeds (groundnuts).

吃（一）把瓜子（花生）吧。

一把剪刀   a pair of scissors

My mother asked me to buy a pair of scissors for her.

我母亲要我给她买一把剪刀。

一把钳子   a pair of tongs

Have you seen a pair of tongs?

你看见一把钳子了吗？

一把铲子   a shovel

He grabbed a shovel and began a ferocious attack on the snowdrift.

他抓起一把铲子对着雪堆猛力地铲起雪来。

一把椅子   a chair

A chair has been fetched for the old man.

已给那位老人拿来了一把椅子。

一把茶壶   a teapot

An old woman walked into the house with a teapot in her hand.

老妇人手中提着一把茶壶走进了屋子。

一把刀子   a knife

The north wind cuts like a knife.

北风象一把刀子那样刺骨。

一把斧头   a hatchet (an axe)

The strong man killed a tiger with a hatchet.

那位身体强壮的人用一把斧头砍死了一只老虎。

一把锄头   a hoe

I have a hoe. I don't know where I have put it.

我有一把锄头，但不知放在哪里了。

一把镰刀   a sickle

The blacksmith beat out the hot iron plate and shaped it into a sickle.

铁匠把烧红的铁板打成一把镰刀。

一把雨伞　an umbrella

He picked up an umbrella and left.

他带着一把雨伞离开了。

They sat under a big umbrella.

他们坐在一把大伞的下面。

(帮)一把　(give or lend someone) a (helping) hand

Instead of exulting over his failure, you should have lent him a helping hand.

你不应该对他的失败幸灾乐祸，而应该帮他一把。

一把汗　breathless with anxiety

Watching him climb up the precipice, everybody was breathless with anxiety.

看见他往悬崖上爬，大家都捏一把汗。

一把年纪　(to be getting on) in years

Tom is getting on in years.

汤姆有一把年纪了。

班　bān

> ①用于人群；②用于定时开行的交通运输工具的班次。

一班······a group of; a class of; a troupe of.

一班年轻人　a group of young people

They are a group of promising young people.

他们是一班很有前途的年轻人。

A group of young people meet at the house every night.

一班年轻人每晚在那屋子里聚会。

一班女孩子 a group of young girls

Also taking part in physical labour are a group of young girls.

参加体力劳动的还有一班女孩子。

一班学生 a class of students

We saw a class of students running outside the building.

我们看见一班学生在大楼外跑步。

一班演员 a troupe of actors (players)

They are a troupe of promising players.

他们是一班很有希望的演员。

一班轮渡 one scheduled run of a ferry

They decided to cut one scheduled run of the ferry.

他们决定停开一班轮渡。

一班飞机 a flight

Is there another flight from Singapore to New York today?

从新加坡到纽约今天还有一班飞机吗?

一班公共汽车 one scheduled run of a bus

There is a Number One bus every five minutes.

一路公共汽车每隔五分钟就有一班。

瓣 bàn

> 用于计算果实、球茎、花瓣等分开的小块数量。

一瓣······**a section of; a segment of; a petal of.**

一瓣蒜　a segment of garlic (a clove of garlic)

She likes to put some segments of garlic in the soup.

她喜欢在汤中放几瓣蒜。

一瓣橘子　an orange

She gave an orange segment to every child.

她给每个孩子一瓣橘子。

一瓣梅花　a petal of plum blossom

That pretty girl has five petals of plum blossoms in her hand.

那位漂亮的女子手中拿着五瓣梅花。

帮　bāng

用于人群, 含褒、贬二义, 与"群、伙"近义。

一帮……a band of; a gang of; a group of.

一帮匪徒　a band of gangsters (a mob of gangsters)

They are searching the woods for a band of gangsters.

他们正在树林中搜寻一帮匪徒。

一帮强盗　a band of robbers

A band of robbers appeared in our town.

我们镇上出现了一帮强盗。

一帮人　a band of men (a gang of men, the gang)

Don't get mixed up with that gang; they spend too much time drinking and gambling.

不要同那一帮人混在一起, 他们整天饮酒赌博。

一帮孩子　a group of children

A group of children gathered around the teacher to ask questions.

一帮孩子围着老师问问题。

包 bāo

用于计算成包物品的数量。

一包……a bale of; a box of; a bundle of; a package of; a pack of; a parcel of; a sack of.

一包棉纱 a bale of cotton yarn
There is a bale of cotton yarn in the way.
有一包棉纱挡住了道路。

一包火柴 a box of matches
Will you please give me a box of matches?
请给我一包火柴好吗？

一包衣服 a bundle of clothes
May I help you with a bundle of clothes?
我帮你拿一包衣服好吗？

一包毛巾 a pack of towels
He was asked to buy a pack of towels for the group.
叫他为该小组买一包毛巾。

一包棉花 a parcel of cotton
A parcel of cotton is not quite heavy.
一包棉花并不是很重的。

一包香烟 a packet of cigarettes (a pack of cigarettes)
He took out a packet of cigarettes and offered me one.
他取出一包香烟，递了一支给我。

一包糖果 a packet of sweets
They made no effort to hide their amusement whenever I produced a packet of sweets from my pocket.

每当我从口袋里拿出一包糖果时，他们就毫不掩饰自己想笑的心情。

一包米　a sack of rice

He is strong enough to carry a sack of rice.

他壮得很，背得动一包米。

抱 bào

> 表示两臂合围的量。

一抱······an armful of

一抱草　an armful of hay

He carried an armful of hay to feed the cows.

他抱了一抱草去给牛吃。

一抱粗　a circumference equal to two arms' length

I can put two arms around that tree.

这棵树有一抱粗。

一抱书　an armful of books

Do you know that man who is carrying an armful of books?

你认识抱着一抱书的那个人吗？

杯 bēi

> 用于计算成杯物品的数量。

一杯······**a cup of; a glass of; a mug of; a tankard of.**

一杯可可　a cup of cocoa

Would you like to have a cup of cocoa?

来一杯可可好吗?

一杯咖啡　a cup of coffee

I used to have a cup of coffee after I got up in the morning.

我过去习惯早上起床后喝一杯咖啡。

一杯茶　a cup of tea

Ordering a cup of tea, I struck up a conversation with the manager.

我要了一杯茶，便和经理攀谈起来。

一杯牛奶　a glass of milk

Prepare a glass of milk for the baby.

为孩子准备一杯牛奶。

一杯水　a glass of water

He felt so thirsty that he had two glasses of water at a time.

他太渴了，一次喝了两杯水。

一杯啤酒　a glass of beer

He likes to have a glass of beer before dinner.

他喜欢在吃饭前喝一杯啤酒。

一大杯啤酒　a tankard of beer (a mug of beer)

He asked me for a meal and a tankard (mug) of beer.

他向我要了一份饭和一大杯啤酒。

本　běn

①用于书籍、簿册等；②用于一定长度的影片。

一本……a book of; a reel of.

一本参考书　a reference book

He was punished for having stolen a reference book.

他因偷了一本参考书而受罚。

一本画册　a book of drawings

Her hand had been playing with a book of drawings, but she now put it down suddenly as if it had burned her.

她的手本来在摆弄着一本画册，但此刻好象被突然烫着了似地把它丢开了。

一本说明书　a book of instructions

Along with each outfit there is a book of instructions.

每套装备附有一本说明书。

一本支票簿　a book of cheques

Miss Zhang put a book of cheques into the drawer and left with the manager.

张小姐把一本支票簿放进抽屉后，便同经理一道离开了。

一本电影　a reel of film

This is a ten-reel film.

这部电影有十本。

一本小说　a novel

This is a novel written by a Frenchman.

这是一位法国人写的一本小说。

一本词典　a dictionary

Please pass me a dictionary.

请递给我一本词典。

一本教科书　a textbook

She sent me a textbook.

她寄给了我一本教科书。

一本杂志   a magazine

He picked up a magazine and began to read.

他拿起一本杂志开始看起来。

笔 bǐ

> ①用于款项或与款项有关的东西；②用于书画艺术。

一笔……a debt of; a sum of.

一笔血债   a debt of blood

It's a debt of blood, and it must be seriously considered.

这是一笔血债，应该严肃考虑。

一笔债务   a debt

John left his son nothing but a debt when he died.

约翰死后留给他儿子的除了一笔债务，别无他物。

一笔巨款   a large sum, a large sum of money

He owed me a sum of money.

他欠我一笔钱。

He paid a large sum for the house.

他花一笔巨款买下了这栋房子。

一笔贷款   a loan

They advanced him a long-term loan.

他们借给了他一笔长期贷款。

一笔生意   a business deal

They have wrapped up a business deal.

他们成交了一笔生意。

一笔养老金   a pension

He got a pension after he retired. (He was given

a pension after he retired.)

他退休后领到一笔养老金。

一笔款子(钱)　a sum of money (a sum)

Tom's uncle sent him a sum of money which enabled him to wipe off his debts.

汤姆的叔父送给他一笔钱，使他得以偿清债务。

一笔好字　good handwriting

"It's really good handwriting!" he said.

"这真是一笔好字!"他说道。

遍 biàn

> 表示动作从开始到结束的整个过程，常置于句末。

一遍　once (one time)

I have read the book twice from cover to cover.

那本书我从头到尾读过两遍。

Please say it again.

请再说一遍。

拨 bō

> 用于人的分组等，与"组"同义，但不及"组"常用。

一拨人　a group of men

There were two groups of men working in the workshop.

车间里有两拨人在工作。

步 bù

> ①指行走时两脚之间的距离；②表示抽象事物，指阶段；③指棋子移动的单位。

一步　a step
　　It's only a few steps away.
　　只有几步远。
　　What's the next step (move)?
　　下一步怎么办？
一步(棋)　a move (in chess)
　　It's an excellent move.
　　这真是一步好棋。

部 bù

> ①用于书籍影片等；②用于机器或车辆。

　　一部……a work of.

一部文学作品　a work of literature
　　He is reading a work of literature.
　　他正在看一部文学作品。
一部美术作品　a work of art
　　The statue is a work of art.
　　这尊雕像是一部美术作品(艺术品)。
一部名著　a classic
　　Robinson Crusoe is a classic.
　　《鲁滨逊飘流记》是一部名著。

一部百科全书　an encyclopaedia

In a sense, an encyclopaedia is a library in itself.

在某种意义上, 一部百科全书本身就是一个图书馆。

一部电影　a film

A new film will be shown tonight.

今晚将上映一部新影片。

一部机器　a machine

This factory has made one hundred drilling machines this year.

这家工厂今年生产了一百部钻机。

一部汽车　a car

He bought a new car.

他买了一部新汽车。

餐　cān

指饭食, 一顿饭为一餐, 与"顿"同义。

一餐饭　a meal

We have three meals a day.

我们一日三餐饭。

册　cè

用于分册的书籍。

一册……**a copy of.**

一册书　a copy of the book

He borrowed a copy of the Bible yesterday.

他昨天借了一册圣经。

100,000 copies of the book have been sold.

这本书已销售十万册。

一册地图集 an atlas

I've lost an atlas that I borrowed from my friend.

我丢失了从朋友那借来的一册地图集。

层 céng

> ①用于物体表面可揭开或抹去的一层东西；
> ②用于重叠积累、梯形等的东西；③用于分项分步的东西。

一层……a bed of; a blanket of; a cloak of; a coat of; a film of; a flake of; a layer of; a line of; a mantle of; a ring of; a tier of; a veil of.

一层泥土 a bed of clay

If you dig here, you will find a bed of clay.

如果你在这儿挖掘，你可以发现一层泥土。

一层土壤 a layer of earth

These seeds must be covered with a layer of earth.

这些种籽上面必须覆盖一层土壤。

一层冰 a layer of ice

It's very cold. There is a layer of ice on the river.

真冷，河面上结了一层冰。

一层岩石 a layer of rock

It's said that there is a layer of rock under the ground.

据说该地下有一层岩石。

一层白灰 a coat of whitewash

He gave the wall a coat of whitewash.

他给这堵墙刷了一层白灰。

You must put another coat of paint on this door.

你应该在这扇门上再涂上一层漆。

一层灰尘　a coat of dust

There is a coat of dust on the desk.

书桌上覆盖着一层灰尘。

一层薄冰　a piece of ice (a thin layer of ice)

We saw pieces of ice floating on the lake.

我们看见湖面上漂浮着一层又一层的薄冰。

一层薄锈　a flake of rust

Flakes of rust are falling from the old iron.

一层层的薄锈从旧铁上脱落。

一层浓雾　a blanket of mist

The valley was covered with a blanket of mist.

山谷被一层浓雾笼罩着。

一层雾　a veil of mist

The trees were hidden in a veil of mist.

树木笼罩在一层雾中。

My eyes seem to have a veil of mist.

我的眼睛里象蒙上了一层雾似的。

一层雪　a mantle of snow (a cloak of snow, a blanket of snow)

There is a mantle of snow on the top of the mountain.

山顶上积了一层雪。

一层塑料薄膜　a film of plastic

You'd better cover it with a film of plastic.

你最好用一层塑料薄膜覆盖住它。

一层油　a film of oil

Seeing a film of oil on the surface of the soup, I felt nausea.

一看到汤面上浮着一层油，我就感到有些恶心。

一层梯田   a tier of terraced field

We saw tiers of (tier upon tier of) terraced fields on the mountain slopes.

我们看到山坡上一层层的梯田。

一层花坛   a tier of flower beds

There are tiers of flower beds on the right side of the road.

大路右边有一层层的花坛。

一层设防   a line of defence

They have set up two lines of defence.

他们已设置了两层设防。

一层火   a ring of fire

They were surrounded by a ring of fire and could not get out.

他们被一层火团团围住，无法逃出来。

一层楼   a floor (a storey)

Our office is on the first floor (美语为second floor).

我们的办公室在二楼。

We plan to erect a building of five storeys (或 a five-storey building,或 a five-storeyed building).

我们打算建一栋五层大楼。

一层意思   an implication

What he said has further implications.

他讲的话还有一层意思。

场 cháng/chǎng

①用于事情的经过；②用于文艺体育活动。

一场······a bout of; a game of.

一场病　a bout of illness

I'm sorry I didn't come to help you last week, because I suffered from a bout of illness.

对不起，上星期我没有来帮助你，因为我生了一场病。

一场流行性感冒　a bout of influenza

What's the matter with you?——I'm suffering from a bout of influenza.

你怎么啦?——我正染上了一场流行性感冒。

一场闹饮（狂饮）　a bout of drinking

After a bout of drinking, they went to the country.

一场狂饮之后，他们便到乡下去了。

一场网球　a game of tennis

What about having a game of tennis?

打一场网球怎么样?

一场球赛　a ball game (a ball match)

There will be a basketball match between Class A and Class B.

甲班与乙班将举行一场篮球赛。

一场音乐会　a concert

There was a concert in Victoria Theatre last Saturday.

上星期六维多利亚剧院有一场音乐会。

一场戏　a play

A new play is being staged in the theatre.

剧院正在上演一场新戏。

一场电影　a film

She was asked to see a film yesterday morning.

昨天上午有人请她去看一场电影。

一场火灾　a fire

A fire broke out during the night.

夜里发生了一场火灾。

一场暴风雪   a snowstorm

A snowstorm is coming up.

一场暴风雪即将来临。

一场大雨   a downpour (heavy rain)

There was a downpour last night.

昨夜下了一场大雨。

车 chē

用于车辆所载的量。

一车……a load of.

一车草   a load of hay

This load of hay will be sent to feed the cows.

这一车草是要送去养牛的。

一车蔬菜   a load of vegetables

They send us a load of vegetables every day.

他们每天帮我们送一车蔬菜来。

一车石头   a load of stones

The truck carried a load of stones to the building site.

卡车载着一车石头驶向建筑工地。

一车木材   a load of wood

Loads of wood were carried from the mountains to the city.

一车车木材从山区运往城市。

一车水泥   a load of cement

They will supply us with a load of cement.

他们将供给我们一车水泥。

一车学生　a car load

A car load of pupils are getting down in front of the school.

一车学生在校门前下车。

匙 chí

用于匙子所盛的量。

一匙……a spoon of.

一匙盐　a spoon of salt

How much salt shall I put in the soup?——Two spoons of salt.

这汤里放多少盐?——两匙盐。

一匙糖　a spoon of sugar

Put a spoon of sugar in the milk.

放一匙糖在牛奶里。

一匙汤　a spoon of soup

"Give the child a spoon of soup," mother said.

"给孩子一匙汤,"母亲说道。

重 chóng

用于分段的东西, 如: 门、山等。

一重门　a door

You will have to pass two successive doors to get there.

你只有经过双重门才能到达那里。

一重山　a mountain

The plane flew over countless mountains.

飞机飞过万重山。

出　chū

用于戏曲中的一个独立剧目。

一出戏　a play

There will be a new play shown in Victoria Theatre tomorrow evening.

明天晚上维多利亚剧院将上演一出新戏。

处　chù

用于某地方或某地方存在的东西。

一处风景优美的地方　a scenic place

I'll take you to a scenic place.

我带你到一处风景优美的地方去玩。

一处人家　a homestead

There were only a few homesteads here some years ago, but now it has become a city of three hundred thousand people.

此地几年前只有几处人家，可现在已成为一座拥有三十万人口的城市。

串　chuàn

用于连串起来的东西。

一串……a bunch of; a cluster of; a rope of; a strand of; a string of.

一串钥匙　a bunch of keys (a string of keys)
She fished out a bunch of keys from her handbag.
她从手提包里掏出一串钥匙来。

一串葡萄　a bunch of grapes (a cluster of grapes)
How much shall I pay for a bunch of grapes?
我买一串葡萄要付多少钱?

一串香蕉　a bunch of bananas
Let's buy a bunch of bananas for the children.
让我们给孩子们买一串香蕉吧。

一串洋葱　a string of onions (a rope of onions)
He came back with a string of onions in his hand.
他回来时，手中提着一串洋葱。

一串珍珠　a rope of pearls (a strand of pearls, a string of pearls)
She had nothing but a rope of pearls.
她除有一串珍珠外，别无它物。

床　chuáng

用于被、褥、蚊帐等。

一床被子　a quilt
My family had no money to buy food, to say nothing of buying a quilt.
我家连买食物的钱都没有，更不用说买一床被子了。

一床毯子　a blanket
He covered himself with a blanket.
他给自己盖上一床毯子。

一床蚊帐　a mosquito net
A mosquito net completely surrounds our bed.
一床蚊帐把我们的床完全罩住了。

次　cì

> 用于事情出现的次数。

一次事故　an accident
The train met with an accident and many passengers were injured.
火车发生了一次事故，许多乘客受了伤。

一次罢工　a strike
Several hundred workers were dismissed by the bosses last week after a strike.
在一次罢工以后，几百名工人上星期被老板开除了。

一次晚会　an evening party
I was asked to attend an evening party.
有人请我参加一次晚会。

一次试验　an experiment
He succeeded only after ten experiments.
他进行了十次试验后才取得成功。

(来过)一次　(be here) one time
Miss Li has been here twice. She wants to have a talk with you.
李小姐来过两次，她想同你谈一谈。

丛　cóng

> 用于生长在一起的草木、毛发等。

一丛……a clump of; a patch of; a thicket;
a tuft of; a tussock of

一丛树　a clump of trees
They will cut down that clump of trees.
他们将把那丛树砍掉。

一丛草　a patch of grass
The snake is crawling towards a patch of grass.
那条蛇正朝一丛草爬去。

一丛毛发　a tuft of hair
Do you know the man with a tuft of hair on the
top of his head?
你认识那个头上长有一丛毛发的人吗？

簇　cù

用于聚集或生长在一起的东西、人群等。

一簇……　a bunch of; a clump of; a cluster of;
a group of; a tuft of; a wisp of.

一簇鲜花　a bunch of flowers (a cluster of flowers)
The small girl was running towards her mother,
with a bunch of flowers in her hand.
那个小女孩子手中拿着一簇鲜花向她母亲跑了过去。

一簇灌木丛　a clump of bushes
The frightened dog hid in a clump of bushes.
那条受惊的狗躲到一簇灌木丛中去了。

一簇草　a tuft of grass
I found it in a tuft of grass where we had been
sitting.
我是在我们坐过的一簇草中找到它的。

一簇人群 a group of people

We saw a group of people singing and dancing on the ground.

我们看见一簇人群在操场上唱歌、跳舞。

撮 cuō

①用于手所撮取的东西；②用于极少数的坏人。

一（小）撮……a handful of; a pinch of.

一撮鼻烟 a pinch of snuff

I wanted another pinch of snuff.

我还要一撮鼻烟。

一撮盐 a pinch of salt

This soup will taste better if you put a pinch of salt in it.

如果你在这汤中放一撮盐，这汤的味道会更好。

一小撮坏人 a handful of bad people

A handful of bad men tried to get out of the country.

一小撮坏人设法逃出这个国家。

打 dá

用于物件，指十二个为一打。

一打……a dozen

一打铅笔 a dozen pencils

He bought a dozen red pencils for his children.

他替孩子们买了一打红色铅笔。

一打红玫瑰　a dozen red roses

Mary wanted to have a dozen red roses.

玛丽想要一打红玫瑰。

代 dài

用于世系的辈分。

一代······a generation of.

一代人　a new generation

A new generation is growing up.

一代新人在成长。

袋 dài

用于袋装的物品。

一袋······a bag of; a pouch of; a sack of

一袋糖果　a bag of candies

Kent, come, here is a bag of candies for you.

过来，肯特，给你一袋糖果。

一袋玩具　a bag of toys

She walked with a bag of toys across the garden in the gray light of the dawn.

她拿着一袋玩具，在晨曦中穿过了花园。

一袋盐　a bag of salt

There is a bag of salt on the table.

餐桌上放着一袋盐。

一袋水泥　a sack of cement

一袋米 a sack of rice

He worked to get some money to buy a sack of rice.

他替老板做工，为的是弄点钱买一袋米。

一袋煤 a sack of coal

I'll help you to carry a sack of coal.

我帮你背一袋煤。

一袋面粉 a sack of flour

What is it?—It's a sack of flour.

这是什么？—— 一袋面粉。

一袋烟 a pouch of tobacco

Take a pouch of tobacco back for your father.

给你父亲带一袋烟回去。

担 dàn

用于成担的东西。

一担……two baskets of; two buckets of; a load of.

一担肥料 a bucket of fertilizer

He fell down by a ditch when he was carrying two buckets of fertilizer.

当他挑（一担）肥料时，不幸跌在沟旁。

一担土(煤) two baskets of clay (coal)

The girl who is carrying two baskets of clay (coal) is my sister.

挑着一担土(煤)的那个女孩是我的妹妹。

一担米 a load of rice

He asked me whether I had seen a man carrying a load of rice.

他问我是否看见一个人挑着一担米。

一担水　two buckets of water

The gardener carried two buckets of water to water the flowers.

园丁挑了一担水浇花。

刀 dāo

①用于一刀切下来的物品；②用于计算纸张的单位。

一刀······**a cut of**

一刀肉　a cut of pork (meat)

I want a nice cut of meat.

我需要一刀上等肉。

一刀纸　one hundred sheets of paper

How much did you pay for one hundred sheets of paper?

你们买一刀纸花去了多少钱?

道 dào

①用于某些长形的东西；　②用于江、河；
③用于所做事情的次数；④用于命令、题目等；　⑤用于门、墙、关卡等。

一道······**a beam of; a coat of; a flash of; a line of; a shaft of; a streak of; a trail of.**

一道亮光   a beam of light (a shaft of light)

A beam of light appeared from behind the curtain.

屏幕后面出现一道亮光。

一道闪光   a shaft of lightning (a streak of lightning, a flash of lightning)

A shaft of lightning suddenly appeared in the darkness.

黑暗中突然出现了一道闪光。

一道脏痕   a streak of dirt

She has a streak of dirt on her face.

她脸上有一道脏痕。

一道漆   a coat of paint

We plan to give these desks two coats of paint.

我们打算给这些书桌上两道漆。

一道长烟   a trail of smoke

The train left a trail of smoke behind it when passing by.

火车从我们旁边驶过，它后面留下一道长烟。

一道防线   a line of defence

We set up a line of defence to guard against enemy attack.

为了防止敌人的进攻，我们建起了一道防线。

一道关卡   a checkpoint (customs)

You have to pass two checkpoints to get there.

你必须经过两道关卡才能到达那个地方。

一道菜   a course

They will serve the first course soon.

他们将送来第一道菜。

一道命令   an order

They must carry out an order given by the authorities.

他们必须执行当局下达的一道命令。

一道河 a river

Our school is near a river.

我们学校靠近一道河。

一道缝 a crack

There is a crack in the door.

门上有一道裂缝。

一道皱纹 a wrinkle

A wrinkle appears on her forehead.

她的额头上出现了一道皱纹。

一道手续 a step (in the process)

If we take his advice, we can save one step in the process.

如果我们采纳他的建议，就可以省一道手续。

一道考题 a question for an examination

Prof. Zhang gave four questions for the examination.

张教授出了四道考题。

一道墙 a wall

We planned to build a wall around the house.

我们计划筑一道墙围住那栋房子。

一道门 a door

There are two doors in this house.

这栋房子有两道门。

滴 dī

用于计算液体滴下的数量。

一滴……a drop of.

一滴水 a drop of water

We mustn't waste a drop of water or a grain of rice.

一滴水一粒米我们都不应当浪费。

一滴油 a drop of oil

He was angry to see a drop of oil on the surface of the table.

看到桌面上有一滴油，他很生气。

一滴雨 a drop of rain

Drops of rain leak from the roof.

从屋顶漏下一滴滴雨水。

一滴血 a drop of blood

The next day in the boat-house the Count caught sight of a drop of blood on the ground.

第二天，伯爵在停船小屋看到地上有一滴血迹。

点 diǎn

用于少量的一点东西。

一点……a bit of; a dash of; a modicum of; a morsel of; an ounce of; a piece of; a speck of; a sprinkling of; a stroke of; a trifle of; a whiff of.

一点水 some water

Give me some water, please.

请给我一点水。

一点英语 a bit of English

He can speak a bit of English.

他能讲一点英语。

一点粉笔 a bit of chalk

I can't find even a bit of chalk.

我连一点粉笔都找不到。

一点建议　a piece of advice

Thank you very much for having given me some good advice.

非常感谢你给我提出了(一点)宝贵建议。

一点好事　a bit of good

It is not difficult to do a bit of good.

一个人做一点好事并不难。

一点胡椒　a dash of pepper

Put in a dash of pepper in the soup.

在这汤里加一点胡椒。

一点糖　a dash of sugar (a bit of sugar)

Tell Mary to put a dash of sugar in the milk and take it to Tom.

告诉玛丽在牛奶里放一点糖，然后给汤姆送去。

一点安慰　a modicum of comfort

Her coming gave me a modicum of comfort.

她的到来给我带来一点安慰。

一点力量　an ounce of strength (a bit of strength)

If I had an ounce of strength, I would have helped you.

如果我有一点力量，我会帮助你的。

一点常识　an ounce of common sense (a morsel of sense)

She hasn't an ounce of common sense.

她一点常识都没有。

He wouldn't do such silly things if he had a morsel of sense.

如果他有一点见识(头脑)的话，他就不会干这样愚蠢的事。

一点灰尘　a speck of dust

It's very clean. You cannot see a speck of dust.

真干净，你看不到一点灰尘。

一点云彩   a speck of cloud

There wasn't a speck of cloud in the sky.

天空中没有一点云彩。

一点牛奶   a speck of milk

There is only a speck of milk left in the bottle.

瓶子里只剩下一点牛奶了。

一点雨   a sprinkling of rain (a bit of rain)

There wasn't a sprinkling of rain in London last month.

上个月伦敦一点雨没下。

一点雪   a sprinkling of snow (a bit of snow)

It was not very cold last winter. We had only a sprinkling of snow.

去年冬天并不十分冷，我们这里只下了一点点雪。

一点运气   a stroke of luck (a piece of luck)

He is a poor fellow. He has never had a stroke of luck.

他真是一个不幸的人，从来没有一点运气。

一点工作   a stroke of work (a bit of work)

Will you please wait for a while? I have a bit of (a stroke of) work to do now.

请等一下，好吗？我现在有一点工作要做。

一点土地   a small piece of land

He used a small piece of land near his house to plant flowers.

他用屋子旁边的一点土地种花。

一点钱   a trifling sum of money (a bit of money, a little money)

The cap cost me a trifling sum of money.

这顶帽子我只花了一点钱。

一点空气　a whiff of air

Every morning he goes out for a walk and a whiff of fresh air.

每天早上，他出去散散步，呼吸一点新鲜空气。

叠 dié

用于折叠堆放在一起的东西。

一叠……a heap of; a pile of; a sheaf of; a wad of.

一叠卡片　a pile of cards

I left a pile of cards on my desk in the office yesterday.

我昨天放了一叠卡片在办公室的办公桌上。

一叠羊毛织品　a pile of woollen goods

The boy lying on top of a pile of woollen goods was Tom.

躺在一叠羊毛织品上的那个男孩是汤姆。

一叠钞票　a wad of bank-notes (a sheaf of bills)

The robber snatched a wad of bank-notes from the cashier.

强盗从出纳员那里抢走了一叠钞票。

一叠信　a wad of letters

A wad of letters arrived today.

今天送来了一叠信件。

一叠纸张　a heap of papers

On the table, beside the little clock, was a heap of papers of various colours.

桌子上，小钟边，摆着一叠五颜六色的纸张。

碟 dié

用于碟装物品。

一碟……a dish of; a plate of.

一碟蔬菜　a dish of vegetables
一碟肉　a plate of meat

Would you like a plate of meat?

No, two dishes of vegetables.

给你来一碟肉好吗?

不, 来两碟蔬菜。

一碟鱼　a plate of fish

How much did you pay for a plate of fish?

你买一碟鱼花了多少钱?

顶 dǐng

用于某些有顶的东西, 如帽子、蚊帐、帐篷等。

一顶帽子　a cap

How I wished I could have a cap, a real soldier's cap!

我多么想有一顶帽子, 一顶真正的军帽!

一顶蚊帐　a mosquito net

I will buy a mosquito net when I get my salary.

我领了薪水后一定去买一顶蚊帐。

一顶帐篷　a tent

There's a tent under the tree. We can have a rest there.

树下有一顶帐篷，我们可在那里休息一下。

锭 dìng

用于某些成锭的东西，常指金、银、药等。

一锭……a tablet of; an ingot of

一锭药　a tablet

The doctor gave her a tablet of aspirin.

医生给了她一锭阿司比灵。

一锭银子　a small ingot of silver

Mary found a small ingot of silver in her room.

玛丽在自己房间里发现了一锭银子。

栋 dòng

用于房屋。

一栋楼房　a building

Some children are playing in front of a building.

一群孩子在一栋楼房前面玩耍。

一栋教学大楼　an institution

A new institution is now under construction.

一栋新的教学大楼正在建造之中。

一栋别墅　a villa

I was told that he had bought a villa.

我听说他买了一栋别墅。

一栋房子 a house

The fireman saved the child just as the house was on the point of collapsing.

消防队员恰好在那栋房子快要倒塌的时候，把小孩救了出来。

堵 dǔ

> 仅用于墙。

一堵墙 a wall

A big wall shut out the light.

一堵高墙把光线挡住了。

度 dù

> 用于所做事情的次数，与"次"同义。

一度会谈 a talk

They hold a talk once a year.

他们一年举行一度会谈。

一年一度的中秋节 the annual Mid-autumn Festival

I decided to spend the annual Mid-autumn Festival with my aunt.

我打算在我姑妈那里欢度一年一度的中秋节。

段 duàn

> ①用于长条东西分成的部分；②用于一定时间、距离等；③用于对话、文章等。

一段……a chunk of; a leg of; a length of; a period of; a piece of; a section of; a streak of.

一段木材(木头)　a chunk of wood (a piece of wood)

A chunk of wood liberates considerable heat during combustion.

当一段木头燃烧时就会放出大量的热。

一段线　a length of wire

Give me a length of wire to bind it.

给我一段线把它捆一下。

一段旅程　a leg of the journey (a section of a journey)

After completing a leg of the journey, we felt very tired.

经过一段旅程后，我们感到非常累。

一段布料　a length of cloth (a piece of cloth)

She bought a length of cloth.

她买了一段布料。

一段管子　a length of pipe (a section of pipe)

Will you help me to find a length of pipe?

你能帮我找一段管子吗?

一段距离　some distance

It's some distance to the station.

到车站有一段距离。

一段历史　a period of history

This period of history falls into two phases.

这一段历史分为两个阶段。

一段路　a section of road (some distance)

A section of the road was damaged by the flood.

洪水冲坏了一段路。

一段时间　a period of time (some time)

John has been watched by the police for a period of time.

约翰已被警方监视了一段时间。

一段走运的时期 a streak of luck

He once had a streak of luck.

他曾经有过一段走运的时期。

一段对话 a dialogue

He asked each of us to make up a dialogue.

他让我们每人编一段对话。

一段情节 an episode

This is an episode from the novel.

这是那部小说中的一段情节。

一段文章 a paragraph

The first paragraph of the article was well written.

这篇文章的第一段写得很好。

堆 duī

> ①用于成堆的物或事; ②用于聚集在一起的人群。

一堆…… a bank of; a crop of; a crowd of; a group of; a heap of; a bundle of; a host of; a mass of; a mountain of; a pile of.

一堆云 a bank of clouds

We passed through a bank of clouds and flew in the direction of New York.

我们穿过一堆云, 朝纽约方向飞去。

一堆雪 a bank of snow (a mass of snow)

There was a bank of snow in the way.

有一堆雪挡住了路。

一堆书 a pile of books

I found it in a pile of books.

我是从一堆书中找到它的。

一堆木料　a pile of logs (wood); a stack of wood

There are piles of logs on the side of the road.

路旁放着一堆堆木料。

一堆灰　a pile of ashes

Nothing is left of a burning log but a pile of ashes.

除一堆灰外，木头燃烧后什么也没有剩下。

一堆砖　a pile of bricks (a heap of bricks)

That pile of bricks in the school garden will be used for building flower beds.

校园里的那一堆砖是用来筑花坛的。

一堆旧报纸　a pile of old newspapers

He rummaged about in the attic and brought out a pile of old newspapers.

他在阁楼里到处翻找，拿出了一堆旧报纸。

一堆物资　a heap of materials

Do not smoke! We are surrounded by heaps of combustible materials.

禁止吸烟！周围是一堆堆易燃物。

一堆石头　a heap of stones

We had to stop here because of the heap of stones in the way.

我们只好停在这儿了，因为一堆石头挡住了去道。

一堆肥料　a heap of manure

They will move a heap of manure away from the road.

他们将把一堆肥料从路上运走。

一堆垃圾　a heap of rubbish

This city is very dirty. Heaps of rubbish can be seen everywhere.

这座城市很脏,到处都可以看到一堆又一堆的垃圾。

一堆衣物　a bundle of clothes

There is a bundle of clothes in a corner of the room.

房角里乱放着一堆衣物。

一堆干草　a pile of hay

The piles of hay in the field have not been removed.

草场上的一堆堆干草还没有清除掉。

一堆书　a pile of books

I saw a pile of books and papers on his desk.

我看见他的书桌上堆放着一堆书和文件。

一堆人　a group of men

These is a group of men eating fish under a tree.

一堆人在树下吃鱼。

一大堆问题　a host of problems (a mountain of problems)

A host of problems has to be dealt with before we actually plunge into the project.

在正式动工以前,我们还有一大堆问题需要解决。

一大堆衣服　a mountain of clothes

She has a mountain of clothes to wash.

她有一大堆衣服要洗。

一大堆工作　a whole stack of work

I cannot go with you now because I have a whole stack of work to do.

现在我不能同你一道去,我有一大堆工作要做。

He has stacks (a whole stack) of work to get through.

他有一大堆工作要完成。

队 duì

> 表示成排的人马、船只、动物等。

一队……a body of; a caravan of; a column of; a fleet of; a flotilla of; a group of; a team of; a train of; a platoon of.

一队学生　a group of students
A group of students marched in the street.
一队学生在街上走着。

一队医生　a team of doctors
A team of docters worked day and night to save his life.
为了抢救他的生命，一队医生夜以继日地工作。

一队骆驼　a caravan of camels
A caravan of camels walked through the desert.
一队骆驼在沙漠上行走。

一队工程师　a team of engineers
He will lead a team of engineers to our factory to improve our technical skills.
他将率领一队工程师到我们工厂来提技术革新。

一队卡车　a fleet of trucks
We saw a fleet of trucks carrying clay to fill a pit.
我们看见一队卡车载着泥土去填坑。

一队船(一个船队)　a fleet of ships
They plan to build a fleet of ships.
他们打算建立一个船队。

一队战舰　a flotilla
There is a flotilla of destroyers heading for the

Indian Ocean.

一队驱逐舰向印度洋开去。

一队蚂蚁 a column of ants

A column of ants were triumphantly bearing an enormous dead beetle home.

一队蚂蚁抬着一只大甲虫凯旋归来。

一队士兵 a column of soldiers

A column of soldiers marched down the road.

一队士兵沿路走了过去。

一队警察 a platoon of police

The authorities sent a platoon of police to the station to keep order.

当局派了一队警察到车站去维持秩序。

对 duì

> 用于成双成对的人、动物或东西等。

一对……a couple of; a brace of; a pair of; a yoke of.

一对夫妇 a couple

They are a newly married couple.

他们是一对新婚夫妇。

一对选手 a couple of players

They are a couple of promising players.

他们是一对很有希望的选手。

一对袜子 a couple of socks

I found a couple of socks in the bedroom but they don't make a pair.

我发现房间里有两只(一对)袜子，但不能成双。

一对兔子　a couple of rabbits (a pair of rabbits)

He came back with a couple of rabbits and a hare.

他回来时，带了一对家兔和一只野兔。

一对鹧鸪　a brace of partridges

He was carrying a bird cage with a brace of partridges in it.

他拿着一个鸟笼，里面有一对鹧鸪。

一对鸟　a brace of birds

The hunter shot a brace of birds.

猎人射中了一对鸟。

一对花瓶　a pair of vases

The auctioneer put up a pair of vases in the late afternoon.

那天傍晚，拍卖商拿出一对花瓶来拍卖。

一对发辫　a pair of pigtails (braids)

She has a pair of beautiful long pigtails.

她有一对漂亮的长辫子。

一对牛(马)　a yoke of oxen (horses)

A yoke of oxen dragged a big log out of the forest.

一对牛把一根大原木从树林中拖出。

墩　dūn

用于丛生的或几棵合在一起的植物。

一墩……**a cluster of.**

一墩草　a cluster of grass

This is but a cluster of grass.

这只不过是一墩草罢了。

一墩稻秧　a cluster of rice seedlings

Up to the present, they have transplanted 5,000 clusters of rice seedlings.

到目前为止，他们已经插了五千墩稻秧。

顿 dùn

> 用于吃饭、发怒、斥责、劝说、打骂等行为的次数。

　一顿……a fit of; a meal of.

一顿饭　a meal

We have three meals a day.

我们一天吃三顿饭。

一顿午饭(早饭、晚饭)　a lunch (a breakfast, a supper)

She managed to prepare a lunch for the unexpected guests.

她设法为那些不速之客准备了一顿午饭。

一顿面条　a meal of noodles

Today's lunch is a meal of noodles.

今天的午餐是一顿面条。

一顿公宴　an official dinner

To be invited to an official dinner given by the Minister was considered an honour by one and all.

能享受部长的一顿公宴，大家引以为荣。

一顿脾气　a fit of temper

His wife flew into a fit of temper before she went to bed.

他妻子在睡觉前，无缘无故地发了一顿脾气。

一顿训斥　a dressing down

The director gave him a dressing down for being late for work again.

由于再次上班迟到，经理训斥了他一顿。

一顿臭骂　a good scolding

Mary gave him a good scolding for having broken the window.

他因打坏了窗子而挨了玛丽的一顿臭骂。

一顿毒打　a good thrashing (a good beating)

朵 duǒ

用于花朵、云彩等。

一朵花　a flower

She picked a flower and put it in her hair.

她采了一朵花插在头发上。

一朵云　a cloud

The curl of smoke in the sky looked like a cloud.

天空中一缕青烟看上去象一朵云似的。

发 fā

用于子弹、炮弹等。

一发……a round of.

一发子弹　a round of cartridge (a bullet)

When he heard a bullet flying over his head, he was very much frightened.

他听见一发子弹从头顶上飞过时，吓坏了。

一发炮弹　a shell

A shell exploded near our office building.

一发炮弹在我们办公大楼附近爆炸了。

番 fān

表示事情的次数或回次。

一番……a piece of; a dose of; a lot of.

一番好意　a kindness

What he said, in fact, is a kindness.

事实上，他所说的是一番好意。

一番奉承　a dose of flattery

He will not be deceived by a dose of flattery.

他不会被一番奉承所蒙骗。

一番功夫　a lot of effort

We learned English with a lot of effort.

我们花了一番功夫学习英语。

一番刺激　a thrill

I got a thrill out of playing the game.

我从这场比赛中得一番刺激。

三番五次　time and again

He asked time and again to go there with us.

他三番五次提出要同我们一道去那里。

方 fāng

①用于立方或平方的东西；②用于方形的东西。

一方······a cubic metre of; a square of; a piece of.

一方木材 a cubic metre of lumber
Our school plans to buy a cubic metre of lumber to repair these chairs.
我们学校打算买一方木材来维修这些椅子。

一方石头 a cubic metre of stones
We need two cubic metres of stones.
我们需要两方石头。

一方土 a cubic metre of earth
They can carry ten cubic metres of earth each day.
他们每天可以运十方土。
〔注〕这里的一方实际上指一立方。

一方地板 a square metre of wooden floor
Tom laid 15 square metres of wooden floor this morning.
汤姆今天上午铺地板十五方。

一方桌布 a tablecloth
My mother bought a tablecloth for ten dollars.
我母亲花了十元买了一方桌布。

分 fēn

用于评定事物的计量单位。

十分把握 a hundred-percent sure
I'm a hundred-percent sure of that.
对那件事情，我有十分把握。

份 fèn

①用于搭配组成的东西，如：食物、礼物等；
②用于报刊、文件等。

一份……a copy of; a helping of; a piece of; a portion of; a list of; a slice of.

一份报纸 a copy of a newspaper
She took a copy of the *New York Times* out of her handbag and began to read.
她从手提包里拿出一份《纽约时报》开始阅读起来。

一份文件 a copy of the document
Make three copies of the document, please.
请把这个文件复制三份。

一份合同 a copy of the contract
Two copies of the contract were made in Chinese and English, both texts being equally valid.
该合同一式两份，每份都用汉语和英语写成，两种文本具有同等效力。

一份条约 a treaty
The ambassador tore up a treaty which was not satisfactory to either nation.
那位大使仓促地草拟了一份条约，结果两国都不满意。

一份煎鱼 a portion of fried fish
I would like to have a portion of fried fish and a bottle of beer.
我想要一份煎鱼和一瓶啤酒。

一份烤鸭 a portion of roast duck

He ordered a portion of roast duck.

他要了一份烤鸭。

一份书单　a list of books

The teacher made out a list of reference books for us.

老师为我们列了一份参考书单。

一份运气　a piece of luck

Thank God for a piece of good luck. At last I was able to buy a gold watch.

感谢上帝赐给我一份好运气，我终于用一点钱买到了一块金表。

一份报告　a report

They have sent out a report to the committee.

他们已给委员会送去了一份报告。

一份提纲　a handout

Before delivering his lecture, the teacher gave each student a handout.

老师在演讲前给每个学生发一份提纲。

一份遗产　an inheritance

Mabel received the inheritance from her aunt.

梅布尔从她姑母那儿继承了一份遗产。

一份目录　a catalogue

He wrote in for a catalogue.

他写信去索取一份目录。

一份电报　a telegram

He came into the room, slapped a telegram down on the desk, and went out without saying a word.

他走进房间，啪的一声把一份电报甩在桌上，一言不发地又出去了。

一份日历　a calendar

Who put a calendar on my desk?

谁放了一份日历在我桌上?

一份礼物 a present

I wish to make you a present in token of my gratitude.

我要送给你一份礼物，以表谢忱。

封 fēng

用于装封袋的东西。

一封信 a letter

They sent us a letter to explain the delay.

他们给我们一封信解释为什么耽搁了。

一封请柬 a letter of invitation

The President sent me a letter of invitation to the White House.

总统给我一封请柬，邀请我到白宫。

幅 fú

用于布帛、呢绒、图画等。

一幅……a piece of.

一幅布料 a piece of cloth

Sew a curtain using two pieces of cloth.

用两幅布料缝个窗帘儿。

一幅画(速写) a picture (a sketch)

He is working up a sketch into a picture.

他正在把一幅速写加工成一幅画。

一幅画(肖像) a portrait

Father hung up a portrait of my grandfather on the wall.

爸爸把一幅祖父的画像挂在墙上。

一幅地图 a map

He opened out a map on the table.

他在桌上摊开一幅地图。

副 fù

> ①用于面部表情;②用于成套或成对的东西。

一副…… a look of; a pack of; a pair of; a set of.

一副无辜的样子 a look of innocence

The bad egg assumed a look of innocence, but it did not take us long to see through him.

那个坏蛋装出一副无辜的样子，但是我们很快就看穿了他。

一副笑脸 a smiling face

一副扑克牌 a pack of playing cards

We found a pack of playing cards and a letter from London in his pocket.

我们在他的衣袋里发现了一副扑克牌和一封来自伦敦的信。

一副拐杖 a pair of crutches

He said he would make a pair of crutches for me.

他说过他会帮我做一副拐杖。

一副眼镜 a pair of glasses (spectacles)

You will look more beautiful if you wear a pair of glasses.

你如果戴上一副眼镜，会显得更漂亮。

一副手套　a pair of gloves

A pair of gloves is a nice present.

一副手套是件好礼物。

一副象棋　a Chinese chess set

I'll borrow a Chinese chess set from him.

我将从他那里借一副象棋。

一副刀叉　a knife and fork

服 fù

用于中药，与"剂"同义。

一服……a dose of.

一服药　a dose of medicine

The doctor advised me to take three doses of traditional Chinese medicine and then come back to be examined again.

医生建议我吃三服中药后再来检查一次。

杆 gǎn

用于有杆的器物。

一杆枪　a rifle

He was running towards the forest, carrying a rifle on his back.

他背着一杆枪跑到林子里去了。

一杆旗　a flag

Everyone has a flag in his hand.

每个人手中拿着一杆旗。

缸 gāng

> 用于陶瓷、搪瓷、玻璃等烧制而成的底小口大的器具所盛的东西。

一缸······a jar of; a vat of.

一缸水　a jar of water
We saw nothing except a jar of water.
除一缸水外，我们什么也没看见。

个 gè

> 用于可数物体或没有专用量词的名词之前，表示数量。

一个······a piece of; a word of.

一个忠告　a piece of advice (a word of advice)
"Let me give you a piece of advice!" said the priest.
"让我给你一个忠告吧！"神父说道。

一个警告　a warning
A sign with "Danger!" on it is a warning.
这上面写着"危险！"的牌示是一个警告。

一个代表团　a delegation
We are delighted to hear that you would like to bring a delegation to our country on a study tour.
我们高兴地获悉，您将率领一个代表团到我国进行考察访问。

一个故事　a story

Please tell us a story.

请给我们讲一个故事吧。

一个问题　a problem (a question)

How to prevent it is a problem.

问题是如何阻止它。

一个晚会　an evening party

To hold an evening party is what he wants most now.

此刻他很想举行一个晚会。

一个苹果　an apple

There, there, don't cry. I'll give you an apple.

好啦，好啦，别哭了。我给你一个苹果。

一个借口　a pretext

This is evidently a pretext.

这很明显是一个借口。

一个帐户　an account

That importer has opened an account with the Bank of China in Singapore.

该进口商在新加坡中国银行开了一个帐户。

根 gēn

用于细长的东西。

一根······a blade of; a branch of; a leaf of; a piece of; a bar of.

一根草　a blade of grass

Who put a blade of grass in the water?

谁放了一根草在水中？

一根树枝　a branch of a tree

He broke off a branch of the tree and carried it off on his bicycle, behaving like a drunkard.

他折断了一根树枝，把它放在一辆自行车上，然后象一个醉汉似地离开了。

一根木料　a piece of wood

I need a piece of wood to repair my desk.

我需要一根木料修理一下我的书桌。

一根柴棍　a piece of firewood

It's said that he died with a piece of firewood in his hand.

据说他死时手中拿着一根柴棍。

一根稻草　a straw

A drowning man will clutch at a straw.

快死的人一根稻草也要抓。（谚语）

一根管子　a tube

The glass was heated and drawn out into a thin tube.

玻璃加热后被拉成一根细管子。

一根棍子　a stick

I managed to beat the dog off with a stick.

我用了一根棍子才算把狗打跑了。

一根绳子　a rope (a piece of string)

They tied his arms behind his back with a rope.

他们用一根绳子把他的手臂绑在背后。

一根链条　a chain

The dog is fastened to a post by a chain.

狗是用一根链条缚在柱子上的。

股 gǔ

①用于风、气体、气味、力气等；②用于成批的人，含贬义；③用于成条的东西。

一股……a blast of; a burst of; a gang of; a gust of; a horde of; a jet of; a puff of; a skein of; a spurt of; a stream of; a trickle of; a whiff of.

一股风 a blast of wind

He passed by me rapidly like a blast of wind.

他从我旁边匆匆而过，就象一股风。

一股热气 a blast of hot air

A blast of hot air came from the furnace.

从火炉那边突然吹来了一股热气。

一股劲 a burst of energy

We completed the work with a final burst of energy.

我们费了一股劲才完成这件事。

一股热情 a burst of enthusiasm

Whatever he does is always with a burst of enthusiasm.

无论干什么，他总是有一股热情。

一股冷气 a gust of cold air

A gust of cold air blew in when he opened the door.

当他打开门，一股冷气吹了出来。

一股寒气 a chill

A chill was striking through his flesh to the marrow of his bones.

一股寒气透过他的皮肉直刺骨髓。

一股凉风 a cool breeze

Suddenly a cool breeze blew in and right away he

felt better.

突然间一股凉风吹了进来，他顿时感觉好了一些。

一股土匪　a gang of bandits

They broke up a gang of bandits deep in the mountains.

他们在深山剿灭了一股土匪。

一股敌军　a horde of enemy soldiers

It's reported that they wiped out a horde of enemy soldiers last night.

据报道，昨晚他们歼灭了一股敌军。

一股毛线　a skein of wool

I paid five dollars for a skein of wool.

买一股毛线我花了五元。

一股怒气　a flash of anger

A flash of anger appeared in her eyes when she found out.

当她知道这件事时，她眼睛里露出一股怒气。

一股尘土　a spurt of earth

His first shot, which fell short, sent up a spurt of earth.

他的第一抢没打中，扬起一股尘土。

一股水　a jet of water

The pipe burst and a jet of water shot across the kitchen.

管子破了，一股水由厨房这边喷到那边。

一股泉水　a stream (a trickle of spring water)

Tears fell like a stream from her eyes.

泪水象一股泉水似地从她眼睛中流了出来。

一股大蒜味　a whiff of garlic

What's the matter? I just caught a whiff of garlic.

怎么回事？我刚才闻到了一股大蒜味。

挂 guà

用于成串的东西，与"串"同义。

一挂……a braid of; a string of.

一挂鞭炮　a string of firecrackers
The boy was running out of the house with a string of firecrackers.
那个男孩拿着一挂鞭炮跑出了屋子。

一挂蒜　a braid of garlic
There was a braid of garlic in the kitchen.
厨房里有一挂蒜。

管 guǎn

用于细长圆筒形的东西。

一管……a tube of.

一管牙膏　a tube of toothpaste
If you are going shopping, please bring back a tube of toothpaste.
要是你上街买东西，请带一管牙膏回来。

一管颜料　a tube of paint
This is not a tube of toothpaste, but a tube of paint.
这不是一管牙膏，而是一管颜料。

一管毛笔　a writing brush
Will you please lend me a writing brush?
请借给我一管毛笔好吗？

罐 guàn

用于罐装物品。

一罐·····a jar of; a jug of.

一罐牛奶　a jug of milk
She put a jug of milk on the table, and left without saying a word.
她把一罐牛奶放在桌上，一言不发地离开了。

一罐果酱　a jar of jam
There is only one jar of apple jam in the refrigerator.
冰箱里只有一罐苹果酱。

一罐水　a jar of water
Please fetch me a jar of water.
请给我去打一罐水来。

一罐米　a jar of rice
She told us that there was a jar of rice on the table.
她告诉我们桌上有一罐米。

锅 guō

用于锅装物品。

一锅·····a cauldron of; a pan of; a pot of.

一锅粥　a cauldron of gruel (a pot of porridge)
There's a cauldron of gruel cooking over the fire.
火上正煮着一锅粥。

一锅汤　a pot of soup

I'm going to cook a pot of soup for them.

我去给他们煮一锅汤。

一锅饺子　a pan of dumplings

She entertained us with a pan of dumplings and some refreshments yesterday.

昨天她用(一锅)饺子和一些茶点来招待我们。

行　háng

用于成行的东西。

一行……a line of; a row of.

一行树　a row of trees (a line of trees)

There are rows of trees in front of our library.

我们图书馆前面有一行行树。

一行诗　a line of verse

I don't understand the first three lines of this verse.

我理解不了这首诗的前三行的含义。

盒　hé

用于盒装物品，包括纸盒、铁盒、塑料盒等。

一盒……a box of; a tin of; a case of; a casket of.

一盒火柴　a box of matches

He was looking for a box of matches.

他东瞧西看地找一盒火柴。

一盒颜料　a box of paints

She sent me a box of paints and a letter which moved me to tears.

她寄给我一盒颜料和一封催人泪下的信。

一盒饼干　a tin of biscuits (crackers)

Take back a tin of biscuits for your children.

带一盒饼干回去给孩子们吃吧。

一盒巧克力　a box of chocolates

He gave every one of the girls a box of chocolates.

他给这些女孩子每人一盒巧克力。

一盒粉笔(钮扣)　a box of chalk

Why do you want a box of chalk?

你要一盒粉笔干什么？

一盒别针　a box of pins

There are two boxes of pins in the drawer; you may have one.

抽屉里有两盒别针，你可以拿一盒去。

一盒宝石　a casket of jewels

He was killed for a casket of jewels three years ago.

三年前，他为一盒宝石而丧了命。

泓 hóng

指清水的一道或一片。

一泓清泉　a clear spring

A clear spring flows from the top of the mountain.

从山顶上流下一泓清泉。

壶 hú

用于壶装物品。

一壶……a kettle of; a pot of.

一壶茶 a pot of tea
Mary went to the forest with a pot of tea in her hand.
玛丽手中提着一壶茶到树林去。

一壶油 a pot of oil
The mouse overturned a pot of oil.
老鼠把一壶油打翻了。

一壶水 a pot of water (a kettle of water)
This is a pot of spring water.
这是一壶泉水。

户 hù

用于人家或住户。

一户人家 a household (a family)
There are thirty households (families) in the village.
全村共三十户人家。

回 huí

①用于书的一章或一个段落部分; ②指事情或动作的次数, 与"次"同义。

一回(指书) a chapter

This novel has 120 chapters.

这部小说共一百二十回。

一回(指动作) one time (once)

He has been here once.

他到这里来过一回。

一回事 a matter

What he said and what he did were entirely different matters.

他所说的和所做的完全是两回事。

伙 huǒ

仅用于人群。

一伙⋯⋯a band of; a gang of; a group of; a mob of; a pack of.

一伙强盗 a band of robbers

A band of robbers inhabit that forest.

一伙强盗住在那林子里。

一伙抢劫犯 a gang of robbers

She shacked up with a gang of bank robbers and ended up by getting killed in a big shoot-out with the police.

她同一伙银行抢劫犯鬼混在一起，终因拒捕被警察击毙。

一伙歹徒 a mob of gangsters

They are pursuing a mob of gangsters.

他们正在追捕一伙歹徒。

一伙小偷 a mob of thieves

They look like a mob of thieves.

他们看上去象一伙小偷似的。

一伙暴徒   a mob of rioters

A mob of rioters rushed into the house and broke everything.

一伙暴徒冲进屋子，打碎了所有的东西。

一伙人   a group of people

A group of people rushed into the house.

一伙人冲进那栋屋子里。

级 jí

①用于台阶、楼梯等；②指质量的等级；
③用于风、地震等。

一级台阶   a step (a stage)

The little girl can walk up a flight of fifty steps in one breath.

那个小女孩一口气能爬五十级台阶。

一级茶   grade A (first class) tea

This is grade A Dragon Well tea sent to me by my Chinese friend.

这是我的一位中国朋友送给我的一级龙井茶。

一级地震   a scale I earthquake

It's reported that a scale Ⅵ earthquake occurred in Japan last night.

据报道，昨晚日本发生了六级地震。

一级风   a force I wind

The well-constructed pavilion on the top of the mountain can not be blown down even by a force 12 wind.

山顶上那座建工精细的亭子即使十二级台风也吹不倒。

记 jì

> 用于打耳光的次数。

一记耳光　a slap in the face
Mary gave him a slap in the face just as he tried to kiss her.
正当他想吻她时，玛丽打了他一记耳光。

剂 jì

> 用于若干味药配合起来的汤药或水药。

一剂……a dose of; a whiff of.

一剂中药　a dose of Chinese herbal medicine
I have to take a dose of Chinese herbal medicine every day.
我每天必须服一剂中药。

一剂麻醉药　a whiff of anaesthetic
The dentist gave her a whiff of anaesthetic.
牙科医生给她注射了一剂麻醉剂。

家 jiā

> 用于家庭或企业单位。

一家人　members of a family (a family)

We are living together like a family.

我们象一家人一样生活在一起。

一家旅馆　a hotel

I ran into an old classmate in a hotel.

我在一家旅馆里偶然碰到了一位老同学。

一家工厂　a factory

He is the manager of a factory

他在一家工厂当经理。

一家饭店　a restaurant

He had gone out to dinner when I called on him.

我去拜访他时，有人请他到一家饭店吃饭去了。

一家公司　a firm

He worked as an interpreter for a firm.

他给一家公司当译员，借此维持生活。

一家出版社　a publishing house

He was once an editor in a publishing house.

他曾经在一家出版社当过编辑。

架 jià

用于有支柱的或有机械装置的东西。

一架钢琴　a piano

A small piano stood against the wall.

有一架小钢琴靠墙放着。

一架照相机　a camera

He was seen taking pictures with a camera.

有人看见他用一架照相机拍照。

一架飞机 a plane (an aeroplane)
We saw a plane flying over the bridge.
我们看见一架飞机从大桥上空飞过。

间 jiān

用于房屋里面的最小单位。

一间房 a room
He rented a room on the first floor.
他在二楼租了一间房。
一间卧室 a bedroom
This room was used as a bedroom before.
这间房过去用作一间卧室。

件 jiàn

用于单个物品或事情。

一件……an article of; a piece of; a stick of; a work of.

一件衣服 an article of clothing
I am wearing several articles of clothing.
我穿了好几件衣服。
一件行李 a piece of luggage
Let me carry a piece of luggage for you.
让我帮你拿一件行李吧!
一件工作 a piece of work (a job)
This is an exhausting piece of work.
这是一件吃力的工作。

一件家具   a piece of furniture

There is only one piece of furniture in the room.

房间里仅有一件家具。

一件瓷器   a piece of china (porcelain)

The boy broke a piece of china yesterday.

昨天那个男孩打破了一件瓷器。

一件艺术品   a work of art

Mike, what a beautiful work of art!

迈克，这是一件多么漂亮的艺术品啊!

一件事情   one thing

I have two things to do this afternoon.

今天下午我有两件事情要做。

节 jié

> 用于分段的东西，文章、课程等。

一节⋯⋯a length of; a section of.

一节管子   a length of pipe (a section of pipe)

Try to get me a length of pipe.

设法帮我弄到一节管子。

一节课   a period (a class)

We'll have two periods this morning.

今天上午我们有两节课。

一节车厢   a railway coach

The policeman told us that he had hidden it in a railway coach.

警察告诉我们他把它藏在一节车厢里了。

截 jié

> 用于分段的东西。

一截……a length of; a section of.

一截电线　a length of wire (a section of wire)

We need another length of wire to connect the two parts.

我还需要一截电线把两部分连接起来。

一截管子　a section of pipe (a length of pipe)

一截木头　a length of log

一截绳子　a length of rope

届 jiè

> 用于定期会议、毕业班级等。

一届会议　one session (one congress)

The Third Session of the U. N. General Assembly was held last year.

第三届联大去年举行。

一届毕业生　a class of graduates

We are not graduates of the same class.

我们不是同一届毕业生。

局 jú

> 用于下棋、玩牌或其它比赛的次数。

一局……a game of; a round of.

一局棋　a game of chess

Whenever he comes here he always asks me to play a game of chess with him.

每当他来这儿时，总是要我同他下一局棋。

一局高尔夫球　a round of golf

Would you like to play a round of golf?

打一局高尔夫球好吗?

一局牌　a round of cards

We have nothing to do now. Let's have a round of cards.

我们现在没有什么事情可做了,让我们玩一局牌吧!

句　jù

仅用于语言。

一句……a line of; a word of.

一句诗　a line of verse

He has never written a line of verse.

他从未写过一句诗。

一句话　a word

I want to have a few words with you.

我想跟你讲几句话。

一句感谢话　a word of thanks

She was so excited that she could hardly say a word of thanks.

她激动得连一句感谢的话也说不出来。

具 jù

用于尸体、棺材或某些器物。

一具尸体　a corpse

She was very much frightened when she saw a corpse.

当她看见一具尸体时，简直吓坏了。

一具座钟　a desk clock

There was nothing left except a desk clock.

除了一具座钟外，什么也没有留下来。

卷 juǎn

用于成卷或卷起来的东西。

一卷……a coil of; a reel of; a roll of; a spool of.

一卷绳子　a coil of rope

The seaman was running over with a coil of rope on his shoulder.

那名海员肩上背着一卷绳子跑了过去。

一卷电线　a coil of wire

Please hand me a coil of wire.

请递给我一卷电线。

一卷线　a reel of thread

Who put a reel of thread on the machine?

谁放了一卷线在这台机器上？

一卷报纸　a roll of newspapers

He took out a roll of newspapers from under his arm.

他从腋下取出一卷报纸。

一卷纸　a roll of paper

Who is the man with a roll of paper in his hand?

手中拿着一卷纸的那个人是谁？

一卷布　a roll of cloth

It's he who left a roll of cloth here yesterday.

就是他昨天放了一卷布在这儿。

一卷地毯　a roll of carpet

How much did you pay for a roll of carpet?

你买一卷地毯花了多少钱？

一卷胶片(软片)　a roll of film (a spool of film)

We used up a whole roll of film.

我们用完了整整一卷胶片。

棵 kē

用于计算植物的数量。

一棵……a head of; a tuft of.

一棵卷心菜　a cabbage

What do you want?——I want a cabbage.

你要点什么？——我要一棵卷心菜。

一棵树　a tree

There is a tree in front of our house.

我们屋子前面有一棵树。

一棵草　a tuft of grass

The tuft of grass on top of the wall sways right and left in the wind.

墙上一棵草，风吹两边倒。

颗 kē

用于星星、子弹，或其它颗粒状的东西。

一颗卫星　a satellite
China sent up another satellite this month.
这个月中国又发射了一颗人造卫星。

一颗流星　a meteor
A meteor suddenly shot across the sky.
一颗流星突然掠过天空。

一颗子弹　a bullet
A bullet glanced off his helmet, but he showed no fear and went on firing at the enemy.
一颗子弹嗖的一声擦过他的钢盔，但他毫无惧色，继续朝着敌人射击。

一颗炸弹　a bomb
一颗糖　a candy (a piece of candy)
一颗珍珠　a pearl
一颗豆子　a bean
一颗沙子　a grain of sand
There's a grain of sand in my left eye.
我左眼里面有一颗沙子。

客 kè

用于食品、饮料等。

一客······a helping of; a portion of.

一客烤牛排 a portion of roast beef (a helping of roast beef)

He was very hungry and ordered two portions of roast beef.

他很饿，所以要了两客烤牛排。

一客冰淇淋 an icecream

I have already had an icecream.

我已用过一客冰淇淋了。

课 kè

用于计算教科书中的单个课文。

一课书 a lesson

This textbook contains 24 lessons.

这本教科书共二十四课。

孔 kǒng

用于窑洞、隧道等。

一孔土窑 a cave

They were found in a cave outside the city.

他们是在城外的一孔土窑中被发现的。

一孔隧道 a tunnel

The government decided to dig a tunnel under the river.

政府决定在这条河下面挖一孔隧道。

口 kǒu

①指一口物品的量；②用于某些东西，如：
井、锅、缸等；③用于人。

一口……a draught of; a morsel of; a mouthful
of; a nip of; a sip of; a whiff of.

一口水 a draught of water
He drank a draught of water and set to work again.
他喝了一口水，又工作起来了。

一口啤酒 a draught of beer
The runners were refreshed with draughts of beer.
喝了几口啤酒后，赛跑运动员恢复了精力。

一口空气 a breath of air
He took a deep breath and said angrily with his
back to me: "I will never believe you again."
他深深地吸了一口气，然后背对着我,生气地说道:
"我再也不会相信你啦。"

一口茶 a mouthful of tea
Talking had made him thirsty, so he hurriedly
swallowed a mouthful of tea and then went straight
into his main theme.
他讲得口渴，连忙喝一口茶，急转直下地转到了正
题。

一口茶(饮料) a sip of tea (drink)
He took a sip of tea.
他呷了一口茶。

一口食物 a morsel of food

I haven't had a morsel of food since I left home.

我从家里出来到现在还没有吃过一口食物（一点东西）呢。

一口白兰地　a nip of brandy

He just took a nip of brandy.

他只是呷了一口白兰地。

一口烟　a puff of a cigarette

He stopped to have a few puffs of the cigarette.

他停下来吸了几口烟。

一口气　a breath

As long as there's a breath left in me, I'll work hard for the company.

只要我还有一口气，就要为公司努力工作。

一口井　a well

They are digging a well.

他们正在挖一口井。

一口锅　a pan (a pot)

I have nothing important to do this morning, so I am going to buy a pan for my parents who are not living with us.

今天上午我没有什么重要事情要做，我打算给父母买一口锅。他们没有和我们生活在一起。

一口人　one person (people)

There are four people in my family.

我家有四口人。

块 kuài

用于块状或某些片状的东西。

一块……an area of; a block of; a cake of; a

chunk of; a handful of; a loaf of; a lump of; a piece of; a plot of; a sheet of; a slab of; a slice of; a tablet of.

一块皮　an area of skin

An area of skin on his hand was burnt away.

他手上的一块皮被烧了。

一块冰　a block of ice

Could I have a block of ice?

我可以拿一块冰吗？

一块肥皂　a cake of soap (a piece of soap, a tablet of soap)

There is a cake of soap in the basin.

脸盆里有一块肥皂。

一块玻璃　a piece of glass

He asked me who broke the piece of glass.

他问我谁打破了一块玻璃。

一块布　a piece of cloth

He spread out a piece of cloth and put the things on it.

他铺上一块布，把东西放在上面。

一块地　a piece of land (a plot, a plot of land)

That piece of land will be used for building a school.

那一块地是要用来建学校的。

一块钢　a piece of steel

A sharp tool can be made from a piece of steel.

一块钢可以制成一件锐利的工具。

一块磁铁　a piece of lodestone

When a piece of lodestone is dipped into iron filings, the filings adhere to it.

把一块磁铁投入铁屑中，铁屑就附着在磁铁上。

一块木头 a piece of wood

A piece of wood can crack without breaking.

一块木头可能会缩裂，但不一定裂成两半。

一块蛋糕 a piece of cake (a slice of cake)

I fancy a cup of coffee and a piece of cake.

我想要一杯咖啡和一块蛋糕。

一块面包 a piece of bread (a loaf of bread, a chunk of bread, a slice of bread)

He satisfied his hunger with a piece of bread.

他吃了一块面包充饥。

一块石头 a piece of rock (a stone)

He picked up a stone and aimed it at the dog.

他捡起一块石头，向狗瞄准。

一块煤 a piece of coal

Put a piece of coal in the stove.

一块煤在炉中。

一块肉 a chunk of meat

Just now I saw a chunk of meat here. Who took it away?

我刚才看见一块肉在这儿呢。谁把它拿走了？

一块骨头 a bone

Two dogs fought for a bone, and a third ran away with it.

两条狗为抢一块骨头而打架，第三条狗把骨头叼走了。

一块石板 a slab of stone

I saw them playing on a slab of stone yesterday.

我昨天看见他们在一块石板上玩耍。

一块黄金 a lump of gold (a gold nugget)

I'll not do it for you even if you give me a gold nugget.

即使你给我一块黄金，我也不会替你干这件事。

一块铅　a lump of lead

The desk is as heavy as a lump of lead.

这张书桌象一块铅一样沉重。

一块粘土　a lump of clay

She has worked a lump of clay into a bust.

她把一块粘土制成一个半身像。

一块砖　a brick

A brick hit him on the head and he was out cold for quite some time.

一块砖头砸在他的头上，他昏迷了好长一段时间。

一块手帕　a handkerchief

He whipped out a handkerchief to bind up his finger.

他抽出一块手帕来包扎手指。

筐　kuāng

用于筐装物品。

一筐······a basket of; a crate of; a hamper of.

一筐苹果　a basket of apples

We bought a basket of apples for the children.

我们为孩子们买了一筐苹果。

一筐鸡蛋　a basket of eggs

Handle with care! This is a basket of eggs.

小心轻放，这是一筐鸡蛋。

一筐鱼　a crate of fish (a basket of fish)

The fishermen gave us a crate of fish when we left.

我们离开那儿时，渔民们送给我们一筐鱼。

一筐衣服　a hamper of clothes

She had to wash two hampers of clothes for them every week.

她必须每周替他们洗两筐衣服。

捆 kǔn

> 用于捆起来的东西。

一捆……a bale of; a bundle of; a sheaf of; a truss of; a wisp of.

一捆纸　a bale of paper

Why do you need two bales of paper?

你要两大捆纸干吗?

一捆棍子　a bundle of of sticks

He went to the river, carrying a bundle of sticks.

他背着一捆棍子朝河边走去。

一捆布　a bale of cloth

When did you leave a bale of cloth here?

你什么时候放了一捆布在这儿呢?

一捆柴火　a bundle of firewood

We saw two boys dragging a bundle of firewood after them.

我们看见两个男孩身后拖着一捆柴火。

一捆麦　a sheaf of wheat

There is only a sheaf of wheat left.

只剩下一捆麦了。

一(小)捆草　a wisp of straw

We saw her going into the house with a wisp of straw in her arms.

我们看见她抱着一(小)捆草走进屋子里。

一捆稻草　a truss of straw (a bundle of hay)
The old man walked slowly to the cowshed, carrying a truss of hay on his back.
老人背着一捆稻草，缓慢地朝牛棚走去。

篮 lán

> 用于篮装物品。

一篮⋯⋯a basket of; a hamper of.

一篮水果　a basket of fruit
They sent me a basket of fruit.
他们送给我一篮水果。

一篮种籽　a basket of seeds
He walked in such a hurry that he turned over a basket of seeds.
他走路如此匆忙，结果把一篮种子给翻了。

一篮鱼　a basket of fish
There are ten baskets of fish by the side of the river.
河边有10篮鱼。

一篮面包　a hamper of bread
Tom asked his father to give a hamper of bread to Mary's family.
汤姆要他父亲送一篮面包给玛丽家。

类 lèi

> 表示种类，用于许多相同的或相似的事物或人，与"种"同义。

一类……a category of; a kind of; a sort of; a type of.

一类问题　a kind of problem
This is another kind of problem.
这属另一类问题。

一类树　a type of tree
This type of tree is easy to grow.
这一类树容易种。

一类人　a sort of person
She was the sort of person to whom deception, when it suited her purpose, never cost a pang.
她是这样一类人：只要适合她的目的，欺诈不引起她半点内疚。

粒 lì

用于粒状物。

一粒……a grain of

一粒米　a grain of rice
We mustn't waste a drop of water or a grain of rice.
一滴水一粒米我们都不应当浪费。

一粒沙子　a grain of sand
There was a grain of sand in my right eye.
我右眼里进了一粒沙子。

一粒子弹　a bullet
A bullet entered his head.
一粒子弹射中了他的脑袋。

一粒钮扣　a button

There are some buttons in the box.
盒子里有几粒钮扣。

连串 lián chuàn

用于行为、事情等，表示一个接一个。

一连串……a chain of; a round of; a streak of; a string of; a round of; a train of; a succession of; a volley of.

一连串事件　a chain of events (a train of events)
A chain of events occurred in our school last week.
上星期我们学校发生了一连串事件。

一连串爆炸　a chain of explosions
The enemy truck caught fire and set off a chain of explosions.
敌人的卡车着了火，引起了一连串爆炸。

一连串反应　a chain of reactions
It is as if a single unimportant event set up a chain of reactions.
似乎一件小事情就会导致一连串的连锁反应。

一连串想法(主意)　a train of ideas
A train of ideas came into my mind after I heard his speech.
听了他的话，我脑海里产生了一连串想法。

一连串胜利(一个又一个的胜利)　a round of victories
We have achieved a round of victories.
我们已经取得了一个又一个的胜利。

一连串晚会(一个接一个的晚会)　a round of parties
She has given a round of parties in the past three

weeks.

在过去了的三周中，她举行了一连串的晚会。

一连串生词   a string of new words

His reading is slowed down by a string of new words.

他的阅读速度由于一连串的生词而慢了下来。

一连串谎言   a string of lies

That's just a string of lies.

那只不过是一连串的谎言罢了。

一连串灾祸   a succession of disasters

Their talk in her room has brought on a succession of disasters.

他俩在她房间的那次谈话带来了一连串的灾祸。

一连串事故   a succession of accidents

A succession of accidents spoiled our trip.

一连串的意外事故干扰了我们的旅行。

一连串问题   a volley of questions (a string of questions)

He asked a volley of questions at the meeting.

他在会上提出了一连串的问题。

辆 liàng

> 仅用于车辆。

一辆警车   a police car

The demonstrators damaged a bus and turned over a police car.

示威群众毁坏了一辆巴士，翻倒了一辆警车。

一辆自行车   a bicycle

He was accused of having stolen a bicycle.

他被指控偷了一辆自行车。

列 liè

仅用于火车。

一列火车　a train
Just then he saw a train approaching.
就在这时候，他看到一列火车开了过来。

一列货车　a cargo train
A cargo train went off the rails not far from here last night.
昨晚有一列货车在离这儿不远的地方出轨了。

令 lǐng

用于原张的纸，表示五百张为一令。

一令……a ream of.

一令纸　a ream of paper
There's a ream of paper in the store and you may take it away.
楼下仓库里有一令纸，你可以拿去。

绺 liǔ

用于头发、胡须、线等细状物的东西。

一绺……a lock of; a skein of; a tuft of; a wisp of.

一绺头发　a lock of hair (a tuft of hair, a wisp of hair)

He was a benevolent-looking person, with a broad forehead adorned like that of Father Time by a single lock of snowy hair.

他是一个容貌慈祥的人，象时光老人那样，宽宽的前额，垂着一绺雪白的卷发。

一绺棉纱　a skein of cotton yarn

一绺丝线　a skein of silk thread

篓 lǒu

用于篓装物品。

一篓······a basket of; a crate of.

一篓废纸　a basket of wastepaper

There are several baskets of wastepaper in front of the factory gate.

工厂大门前有几篓废纸。

一篓瓶子　a crate of bottles

She was very angry to see a crate of empty bottles in a corner of the room.

她看到房角有一篓空瓶子，十分生气。

炉 lú

用于炉子所烤或炼的东西。

一炉······a batch of; a cast.

一炉面包　a batch of bread

She baked a batch of bread for us.

她为我们烤了一炉面包。

一炉钢　a cast of steel

After that they were able to cut down the time for casting steel by some 20 minutes.

在这之后，他们就能把炼一炉钢的时间缩短了约二十分钟。

缕 lǚ

> 用于长形的东西，如光线、烟雾等。

一缕……a curl of; a strand of; a stream of; a trail of; a wisp of.

一缕光线　a stream of light

A stream of light suddenly came out of the window.

突然从窗口射出一缕光线。

一缕麻　a strand of hemp

Tom, your father wants you to buy a strand of hemp.

汤姆，你父亲叫你去买一缕麻。

一缕烟　a wisp of smoke (a trail of smoke, a curl of smoke)

A wisp of smoke is curling up from the kitchen chimney.

一缕炊烟袅袅上升。

轮 lún

> ①用于循环的事物或动作；②用于红日、明月等。

一轮……a round of.

一轮会谈　a round of talks

This is their first round of talks.

这是他们的第一轮会谈。

一轮比赛　a round of matches (a round of the tournament)

He drew a bye in the first round of the tournament.

他在第一轮比赛中轮空。

一轮明月　a bright moon

A bright moon hung in the sky.

天上挂着一轮明月。

罗 luó

> 指物品的十二打为一罗，属商业用语。

一罗……a gross of.

一罗铅笔　a gross of pencils

How much does a gross of pencils cost?

一罗铅笔要多少钱?

一罗瓶子　a gross of bottles

There is a gross of bottles in front of the shop.

店子门前有一罗瓶子。

码 mǎ

> ①用于计算布的数量; ②用于一件或一类事情。

一码布　a yard of cloth

This tablecloth was made out of a yard of cloth.

这块台布是用一码布做成的。

一码事　the same thing

What you said is not the same thing as what he said.

你说的与他说的不是一码事。

枚　méi

> 多用于体形小的东西或水雷、火箭之类的东西。

一枚水雷　a mine

The ship's bow was blown off by a mine.

船头被一枚水雷炸掉了。

一枚照明弹　a flare

The distressed ship sent up a flare.

遇难的轮船发射了一枚照明弹。

一枚火箭　a rocket

In 1969, the United States succeeded in sending a rocket to the moon.

一九六九年，美国成功地把一枚火箭送上了月球。

一枚校徽　a school badge

Every student has got a school badge.

每个学生都有一枚校徽。

门　mén

> ①用于炮；②用于技术、功课等。

一门……a branch of; a piece of.

一门炮　a piece of artillery (a cannon)

What a fine piece of artillery!

这是多好的一门炮啊！

一门科学　a science (a branch of knowledge)

Astronomy is a science that is concerned with the movement of heavenly bodies.

天文学是一门涉及天体运动的科学。

一门课　a course (a subject)

They offered an advanced English course.

他们开设了一门高级英语课。

面　miàn

①多用于扁平的物件；②用于见面的次数。

一面旗子　a flag

The man signalled with a flag at the railway crossing.

那人在铁路交叉处用一面旗子打信号。

一面镜子　a mirror

A woman usually carries a small mirror in her bag.

妇女常常在手提包里放一面小镜子随身带着。

(见过)一面　(meet somebody) once

I met her twice.

我见过她两面。

名　míng

用于有职务的人。

一名教师　a teacher

It's easy to be a teacher, but it is difficult to be a good teacher.

当一名教师并不难，然而当一名好教师却不是一件容易的事。

一名工人　a worker

He was a worker before, but now he is a writer.

他过去是一名工人，可现在是一名作家。

幕 mù

用于戏剧较完整的段落或情景的场面。

一幕戏　an act

This is the first act; the second will start two minutes later.

这是第一幕；第二幕两分钟后开始。

一幕动人的景象　a moving scene

Before our eyes appears a moving scene.

展现在我们面前的是一幕动人的景象。

排 pái

用于成行列的东西或人。

一排……a block of; a line of; a range of; a rank of; a row of; a screen of.

一排建筑物　a block of buildings (a line of buildings, a row of buildings)

In order to build the highway, the constructors had to tear down a whole block of buildings.

为了修那条高速公路，筑路工人不得不将一排建筑物全部拆除。

一排桌子 a line of desks

There is a line of desks against the wall.

有一排桌子靠墙放着。

一排树 a row of trees

They were both walking along the gravelled path beside a row of cypresses.

他俩在一条穿过一排柏树的石子路上走着。

一排珠子 a row of beads

On an abacus each row of beads represents a different number.

在算盘上一排排珠子代表数字。

一排房屋 a row of houses

Rows of houses are under construction.

一排排的房屋正在修建之中。

一排战士 a rank of soldiers

I saw a rank of soldiers practising shooting.

我看见一排战士在练习射击。

一排机器 a rank of machines

Ranks of textile machines are running at full blast.

一排排的纺纱机正在全速运转。

一排座位 a row of seats

There is row of seats for the foreigners in the stadium.

看台上为外宾安排了一排座位。

派 pài

用于语言、声音、景色等。

一派……**a pack of.**

一派胡言　a pack of nonsense

What he said is only a pack of nonsense.

他所说的只不过是一派胡言。

一派谎言　a pack of lies

No one will believe your pack of lies.

谁也不会相信你的一派谎言。

一派节日气象　a festive air

The city took on a festive air.

全城呈现一派节日气象。

盘　pán

①用于盘状形的东西；②用于盘装物品。

一盘……**a coil of; a dish of; a game of; a plate of.**

一盘蚊香　a mosquite coil

He burnt a mosquito coil to keep off the mosquitoes.

他点着一盘蚊香以驱赶蚊子。

一盘鱼　a plate of fish

I want a plate of fish and two plates of beef.

给我来一盘鱼、两盘牛肉。

一盘棋　a game of chess

Let's have a game of chess.

我们下一盘棋吧。

泡 pāo

用于尿屎。

一泡尿　(pass) water
The baby wet the bed three times last night.
小孩昨晚拉了三泡尿在床上（湿了三次床）。

盆 pén

用于盆装物品。

一盆……**a basin of; a bowl of; a pot of; a tub of.**

一盆水　a basin of water (a tub of water)
He asked me to fetch him a basin of water.
他要我去给他打一盆水来。

一盆花　a pot of flowers
A pot of flowers can make a room attractive.
一盆花可以使房间显得漂亮。

一盆金鱼　a bowl of goldfish
I bought a bowl of goldfish yesterday.
昨天我买了一盆金鱼。

蓬 péng

用于枝叶茂盛的花草等。

一蓬……**a clump of.**

一蓬竹子　a clump of bamboo

There is a clump of bamboo in their garden.

他们花园里有一蓬竹子。

捧　pěng

用于双手捧着的东西。

一捧……a double handful of.

一捧花生　a double handful of peanuts

Jane went out of the room, holding a double handful of peanuts.

珍捧着一捧花生走出房间。

一捧米　a double handful of rice

Feed the chickens with a double handful of rice.

用一捧米喂鸡。

批　pī

用于大宗货物或多数的人群。

一批……　an array of; an assortment of; a batch of; a body of; a crop of; a galaxy of; a group of; a muster of; a number of; a party of; a set of; a stock of; a supply of.

一批工具　an array of tools

He showed us an array of tools.

他给我看了一批工具。

一批货物　an assortment of goods

We have imported an assortment of cloth from America.

我们已经从美国进口了一批花色齐全的布料。

一批通知　a batch of circulars

My personal letters got muddled up with a batch of circulars.

我的私人信件和一批通知混在一起了。

一批书　a batch of books

I still owe payment for my last batch of books.

最后一批书的钱我还没有付。

一批来访者　a batch of visitors (a party of visitors)

There's a fresh batch of visitors in our school.

我们学校新到了一批来访者。

一批人　a number of people (a body of people, a group of people)

Large numbers of people were standing around the house.

房子周围围着大批人。

一批失业者　a body of unemployed men

A large body of unemployed men went to the industrial area to look for work.

一大批失业者到工业区去找工作。

一批画　a batch of paintings

The museum exhibited a batch of modern paintings.

博物馆展出了一批现代画。

一批护士　a batch of nurses

A large hospital has to have a batch of experienced nurses.

一所大医院必须有一批有经验的护士。

一批医生　a group of doctors

A group of doctors arrived to inoculate the recruits.

来了一批医生给新兵注射预防针。

一批选手 a team of players

They were a team of promising table tennis players.

他们是一批大有希望的乒乓球选手。

一批武士 a galaxy of knights

The queen was followed by a galaxy of brave knights and fair ladies.

女王身后跟随着一批勇敢的武士和美丽的贵妇。

一批工人 a group of workers

These veteran workers have undertaken to train a group of young workers.

这些老工人负责培养一批青年工人。

一批学生 a group of students (a number of students)

The calculator was made by a group of students.

这部计算机是一批学生制造的。

一批作家 a group of writers

He was introduced to a group of writers.

他被介绍给一批作家认识。

一批小学生 a party of school children

It is said that a party of school children would go to France.

据说一批小学生将到法国去。

一批笔记 a set of notes

He is writing a set of notes for the examination.

他正在整理一批笔记，准备应付考试。

一批五金存货 a stock of hardware

This store keeps a large stock of hardware.

这店里备有一大批五金存货。

一批燃料 a supply of fuel

We have a large supply of fuel.

我们有一大批燃料供应。

匹 pǐ

①用于整卷的绸或布; ②用于马、骡等。

一匹……a bolt of; a roll of.

一匹布 a bolt of cloth (a roll of cloth)
They produce over 1,000 bolts of cloth weekly.
他们每周生产一千多匹布。

一匹驴子 a donkey
A donkey is drawing a cart.
一匹驴子正在拉车。

一匹马 a horse
Both in school and at home, she was like an
unbridled wild horse.
在学校里, 在家里, 她象一匹脱缰的野马。

篇 piān

用于文章、纸张、书页等。

一篇……a piece of; a sheet of.

一篇文章 a piece of writing (an article)
This is a good piece of writing.
这是一篇好文章。

一篇乐谱 a sheet of music (a piece of music)
He tore up sheet after sheet of music before
producing the happy tune he wanted.

他撕掉一篇又一篇的乐谱，最后他才写出他想要的合适的调子。

一篇报道　a report

He whipped up a report in half an hour.

半小时之内，他匆匆写完了一篇报道。

一篇作文　a composition

Every student has to hand in a composition in English.

每个学生都要交一篇用英文写的作文。

一篇故事　a story

She was reading a story to the children.

她那时正在给孩子们念一篇故事。

片　piàn

①用于成片的东西；②用于地面、水面等；
③用于景色、气象、声音、语言、心意等。

一片……an area of; a blanket of; a blaze of; a body of; an expanse of; a flood of; a mass of; a scene of; a sea of; a sheet of; a slice of; a stretch of; a tract of; a petal.

一片白雪　a blanket of snow

There was a blanket of snow on the top of the mountain.

山顶上有一片白雪。

一片水　a body of water (a stretch of water)

The mountaineering party found a body of water on top of the high plateau.

爬山队在山顶上发现了一片水。

一片月光　a flood of moonlight

The moon came up from behind the hills and bathed the village in a flood of light.

月亮从山后升起，全村沐浴在一片月光之中。

一片色彩　a mass of colour

The azaleas made a mass of colour in the garden.

杜鹃花给花园增添了一片色彩。

一片沸腾　a blaze of excitement

The whole factory was in a blaze of excitement over the delegates' arrival.

由于代表团的到来，全厂一片沸腾。

一片欢腾　a great cheer (a scene of great rejoicing)

When the floats appeared, a great cheer went up.

当花车出现时，顿时一片欢腾。

一片混乱　a scene of confusion (a state of chaos)

Looking into the drawing room, she saw a scene of confusion.

她向客厅望去，只见一片混乱。

一片繁忙景象　a scene of bustling activity

The advent of the New Year is a scene of bustling activity everywhere.

随着新年的来临，到处呈现一片繁忙的景象。

一片汪洋　a vast expanse of water

In his writing he often compared the endless sand to a vast expanse of water.

在他的作品中，他时常把无际的沙漠比着一片汪洋。

一片火海　a sheet of flames

The whole village was a sheet of flames because of the fire.

由于发生火灾，整个村庄处在一片火海之中。

一片面包　a slice of bread

She never had much for breakfast. She would drink a cup of coffee and nibble at a slice of bread.

她早饭一向吃得不多, 通常喝一杯咖啡, 吃一片面包。

一片花瓣　a petal

I only found a petal.

我只发现了一片花瓣。

一片干酪　a piece of cheese

Just a piece of cheese and a slice of bread.

请来一片干酪和一片面包。

一片稻子　fields of rice

Vast golden fields of rice were waiting to be cut.

一大片金黄的稻子等着收割。

一片土地　a stretch of land

A wide stretch of land spread out in front of us.

一片广阔的土地展现在我们面前。

一片平原　a stretch of plain

After we have climbed over the mountain, we saw a stretch of plain before us.

翻过一座大山, 展现在我们面前的是一片平原。

一片旷野　a stretch of open country

We drove to a stretch of open country to see whether we could build a factory there.

我们驱车前往一片旷野, 看看是否能在那儿建一家工厂。

一片沙漠　a great tract of sand

When I woke at midnight, what I saw was a great tract of sand.

当我半夜醒来, 看到的却是一片沙漠。

一片草地(牧地)　a meadow

After walking for two days, we reached a meadow.

经过两天的步行后，我们到达一片牧地。

一片脚步声 a patter of footsteps

Suddenly a patter of footsteps sounded upstairs.

突然楼上出现一片脚步声。

一片药 a tablet

The doctor advised me to take two sleeping tablets every evening.

医生建议我每天晚上服两片安眠药。

撇 piě

一撇眉毛 a brow

He looks very handsome, with two bushy brows over a pair of big eyes.

他显得十分英俊，生着两撇浓眉，一双大眼。

一撇胡子 a moustache

Do you know that man with the moustache?

你认识那个嘴上留着一撇胡子的人吗？

瓶 píng

用于瓶装物品。

一瓶······a bottle of; a flask of.

一瓶啤酒 a bottle of beer

He can gulp a bottle of beer down in one draught.

他可以一口气喝光一瓶啤酒。

一瓶香水 a bottle of perfume

She wants me to buy her a bottle of perfume.

她要我给她买一瓶香水。

一瓶水　a flask of water (a bottle of water)

Ask him to fetch me a flask of water.

叫他去给我打一瓶水来。

期　qī

> 用于期刊，杂志或分期的事物。

一期……an issue of; a class ot; a period of; a phase of; a term of.

一期《欢乐园》　an issue of *Happy Paradise*

I bought the third issue of *Happy Paradise*.

我买了第三期《欢乐园》。

一期毕业生　a class of graduates

We are graduates of the same class.

我们是同一期毕业生。

一期工程　a phase of the project

The first phase of the project will be finished next month.

第一期工程下个月完成。

一期训练班　a training course

We have run three English training courses.

我们办了三期英语训练班。

起　qǐ

> 用于事情发生的件数或次数。

一起……a case of.

一起谋杀案 a case of murder

The evidence all adds up to a case of murder.

所有证据都说明这是一起谋杀案。

一起火警 a case of fire alarm

There were three cases of fire alarm in the factory.

这家工厂曾经发生过三起火警。

群 qún

用于成群的人、动物、生物等。

一群……a circle of; a company of; a congre-gation of; a crowd of; a drove of; a flight of; a flock of; a gaggle of; a bevy of; a gang of; a group of; a herd of; a swarm of; a horde of; a host of; a huddle; a mob of; a multitude of; a pack of; a party of; a pride of; a school of; a shoal of; a galaxy of; a throng of; a troop of; a troupe of; a rabble of.

一群女孩 a group of girls

We saw a group of girls dancing over there.

我们看见一群女孩在那儿跳舞。

一群朋友 a circle of friends

He has a circle of friends who are interested in music.

他有一群爱好音乐的朋友。

一群苍蝇 a swarm of flies

There are swarms of flies everywhere.

到处是一群群的苍蝇。

一群建筑物 blocks of buildings

There are blocks of buidings around our school.

我们学校周围是一群群建筑物。

一群蝴蝶 a cluster of butterflies

Clusters of butterflies are flying here and there in the garden.

一群群蝴蝶在花园里飞来飞去。

一群参观者 a party of visitors (a group of visitors)

I will show a party of visitors around the factory.

我将领一群参观者参观工厂。

一群旅客 a party of travellers

A great party of travellers were injured in a train accident.

在一次火车事故中，一大群旅客受了伤。

一群崇拜者 a congregation

He has his own congregation.

他自有一群崇拜者。

一群孩子 a group of children

The door opened and in came a group of children.

门一开，一群孩子就涌了进来。

一群马 a drove of horses

We saw a drove of horses running by the side of the river.

我们看见一群马在河边奔跑。

一群飞雀 a flight of sparrows

Tom mistook a flight of sparrows for a flight of swallows.

汤姆错把一群飞雀当作一群飞燕了。

一群羊 a flock of sheep

A flock of sheep eating grass ranged over the mountain slope.

一群羊在山坡上吃草。

一群野鸭　a flock of wild ducks

A flock of wild ducks are swimming in the river.

一群野鸭在河里游着。

一群鹅　a gaggle of geese

His father keeps a gaggle of geese.

他父亲养了一群鹅。

一群美女　a bevy of beautiful women

Wherever the king went, he was followed by a bevy of beautiful women.

国王无论走到哪里，身后总是跟着一群美女。

一群暴徒　a gang of roughs

The boy was beaten up by a gang of roughs until he was black and blue.

那个男孩被一群暴徒打得青一块紫一块。

一群警察　a posse of policemen (an array of policemen)

A posse of policemen battled with the rioters.

一大群警察与暴民冲突。

一群人　a group of people (a crowd, a mob of people, a throng of people)

They noticed a crowd of people shouting and cheering.

他们看到一群人在叫喊欢呼。

一群蜜蜂　a swarm of bees

Mary was very much frightened when she saw a swarm of bees.

玛丽看到一群蜜蜂，被吓坏了。

一群牛　a herd of cows

We saw a herd of cows watched by a herdsman on horse-back.

我们看到一个骑马的牧民放牧着一群牛。

一群鹿 a herd of deer

A pack of wolves were running after a herd of deer.

一群狼正在追捕一群鹿。

一群流氓 a gang of ruffians

She was badly beaten up by a gang of ruffians.

她被一群流氓打成重伤。

一群狼 a pack of wolves

We saw a pack of wolves running into the forest.

我们看见一群狼跑进树林里去了。

一群猎犬 a pack of hounds

The policemen are training a pack of hounds in the field.

警察正在野外训练一群猎犬。

一群狮子 a pride of lions

I saw a pride of lions in the grasslands.

我在草原中发现了一群狮子。

一群鲸鱼 a school of whales

They are studying the life of a school of whales.

他们正在研究一群鲸鱼的生活习性。

一群鱼 a shoal of fish

Shoals of fish died because of water pollution.

成群的鱼死于水污染。

一群蚂蚁 a swarm of ants

A swarm of ants scattered in all directions.

一群蚂蚁向四处逃散。

一群演员 a troupe of actors

A troupe of actors were drinking and dancing upstairs.

一群演员在楼上寻欢作乐。

一群猴子 a troop of monkeys

We saw a troop of monkeys running into the forest.
我们看见一群猴子跑进了树林。

任 rèn

> 用于担任官职的次数。

一任校长　(be) a principal once
He was the second principal of the school.
他是学校的第二任校长。

扇 shàn

> 用于门、窗等。

一扇门　a door
There is a door at the side of the house.
屋子的侧面有一扇门。
一扇窗子　a window
The thief broke a window, climbed out and ran away.
小偷砸破了一扇窗子，越窗逃走了。

身 shēn

> 用于成套衣服或身躯上面的东西。

一身冷汗　a cold sweat
This made me break out in a cold sweat.
这吓得我出了一身冷汗。
一身衣服　a suit (of clothes)

She is going to change into her new suit.

她去换一身新衣服。

声　shēng

> 用于发出声响的次数。

一声枪响　a shot

As soon as he heard a shot he ran out of the room.

他听到一声枪响，就马上跑出房间。

一声叫喊　a call (a cry)

She let out an agonized cry.

她发出一声叫喊。

手　shǒu

> 用于技能、本领等。

一手好手艺　a master of the craft

He's a master of his craft.

他有一手好手艺。

一手好字　good handwriting

He was employed because he has good handwriting.

他因写得一手好字而受雇。

首　shǒu

> 用于诗、歌等。

一首歌　a song

They finally prevailed upon her to sing a folk song for them.

他们终于使得她同意给他们唱一首民歌。

一首诗　a poem

He showed me a poem he had written and asked my opinion about it.

他给我看了他写的一首诗，要我提意见。

束 shù

用于捆在一起的小把东西。

一束……a beam of; a bouquet of; a bunch of; a cluster of; a hank of; a bundle of.

一束光　a beam of light

A searchlight or a flashlight sends out a beam of light.

探照灯或电筒能发出一束光来。

一束鲜花　a bunch of flowers (a bouquet of flowers)

They presented him with a bouquet of flowers.

他们献给他一束鲜花。

一束毛线　a hank of wool

She put a hank of wool into her handbag, took out a book and began to read.

她把一束毛线放进手提包里，拿出一本书，开始阅读起来。

双 shuāng

用于相匹配的成对的东西。

一双······a pair of.

一双鞋子   a pair of shoes
A pair of shoes is a nice present.
一双鞋是件好礼品。
一双手套   a pair of gloves
I left a pair of gloves in the classroom.
我丢了一双手套在教室里了。
一双筷子   a pair of chopsticks
一双靴子   a pair of boots

丝 sī

用于极小或极少量的丝状形的东西。

一丝······a breath of; a flicker of.

一丝风   a breath of wind
It's really very hot today. There isn't a breath of
wind even in the morning.
今天真热，就是早上也没有一丝儿风。
一丝怀疑   a flicker of doubt
There was just a flicker of doubt in her mind.
她脑海里仅闪过一丝怀疑。
一丝笑容   a smile
Gradually a smile appeared on her face.
慢慢地她脸上露出一丝笑容。

艘 sōu

用于较大的船只。

一艘轮船 a ship

We salvaged a ship that went on the rocks some thirty years ago.

我们打捞了一艘三十年前触礁沉没的轮船。

一艘油轮 a tanker

A tanker rammed into a fishing boat and capsized it.

一条鱼船被一艘油轮撞沉了。

岁 suì

指年龄单位。

一岁孩子 a one-year-old child

He is ten years old now.

他现在十岁了。

所 suǒ

①用于学校、医院等事业单位；②用于房屋，与"栋"同义。

一所学校 a school

一所医院 a hospital

The government has built a new hospital.

政府建了一所新医院。

一所房子 a house

At last they were able to afford a house.

他们终于有钱买一所房子了。

胎 tāi

> 用于怀孕或生育的次数。

一胎　a farrow (a birth)
This sow has twelve piglets at one farrow (one birth).
这头母猪一胎下了十二头小猪。

台 tái

> 用于机电装置或演戏的台数。

一台录音机　a recorder
The father agreed to buy his son a recorder.
父亲同意给儿子买一台录音机。

一台电视机　a television set
We pitched in to buy a television set.
我们出钱合买了一台电视机。

一台电扇　an electric fan
We have only one electric fan in our office.
我们办公室里只有一台电扇。

一台显微镜　a microscope
They will supply us with a microscope.
他们将给我们提供一台显微镜。

一台机器　a machine

一台戏　a theatrical performance

摊　tān

用于摊开的糊状物。

一摊……a pool of; a puddle of.

一摊水　a pool of water (a puddle of water)
There's a pool of water in the garden. You must try to get rid of it as quickly as possible.
花园里有一摊水，你必须尽快处理掉。

一摊血　a pool of blood
There's a pool of blood on the ground. Someone must have died in the bus accident.
地上有一摊血，一定有人死于车祸了。

堂　táng

①用于分节的课程；②用于成套的家具。

一堂……a period of; a set of.

一堂课　a period (a class)
There will be a class in physics tomorrow morning.
明天上午有一堂物理课。

一堂家具　a set of furniture
They bought a set of furniture on hire purchase.
他们以分期付款的方式买了一堂家具。

趟　tàng

①用于成行的东西；②用于走动的次数。

一趟……a row of.

一趟街　a street

Take this way; cross two streets and you will get to the station.

走这条路，穿过两趟街，就可以到达车站。

一趟飞机　a flight (an airliner)

There is a flight from Singapore to New York in the afternoon.

今天下午从新加坡到纽约有一趟班机。

一趟火车　a train

There is another train going to London today.

今天还有一趟火车开往伦敦。

套 tào

用于成组的东西或事情。

一套……an article of; a set of; a pack of.

一套衣服　a suit

I want you to measure me for a new suit of clothes.

我想请你量一量尺寸，我要做一套新衣服。

一套邮票　a set of stamps

The boy is itching for a set of the new stamps.

那个男孩渴望得到一套这样的新邮票。

一套规则(条文)　a set of rules

As has been said before, grammar is not a set of dead rules.

从前讲过，语法并不是一套死规则。

一套书　a set of books

He ordered himself a set of encyclopaedia.

他定购了一套百科全书。

一套仪器　a set of apparatus

He used a set of apparatus to demonstrate that water is made of hydrogen and oxygen.

他用一套仪器做实验，说明水是由氢和氧组成的。

一套碗盏　a set of dishes

She completed her set of dishes by buying the cups and saucers.

她买了些杯、碟，把她的一套碗盏配齐了。

一套设备　a set of equipment

The factory imported a set of equipment from Japan.

这家工厂从日本进口了一套设备。

一套谎言　a pack of lies

She fabricated a pack of lies to deceive her husband.

她编造了一套谎言来欺骗她的丈夫。

条　tiáo

①用于以固定数量合成的某些长条形的东西或自成形的细长东西；②用于分项的事物。

一条……a bar of; a carton of; an item of; a loaf of; a pair of; a piece of.

一条肥皂　a bar of soap

I am going to buy a bar of soap and shall be back soon.

我去买一条肥皂，很快就回来。

一条香烟　a carton of cigarettes

I'll give you a carton of cigarettes.

我将给你一条香烟。

一条面包　a loaf of bread

He asked me for a loaf of bread and a tankard of beer.

他向我要了一条面包和一大杯啤酒。

一条裤子　a pair of trousers

This piece of material can be made into a pair of trousers.

这段布料可以裁成一条裤子。

一条新闻(消息)　a piece of news (an item of news)

I have a piece of news to tell you.

我有一条消息要告诉你们。

一条路　a road

The dam is approached by a broad road.

沿着一条宽阔的马路可到达学校。

一条领带　a tie

Will you help to choose a new tie for me?

你能帮我挑一条新领带吗?

一条披巾　a shawl

She wore a white shawl over her shoulder.

她肩上披着一条白色的披巾。

一条手帕　a handkerchief

He whipped out a handkerchief to bind up his injured finger.

他掏出一条手帕将受伤的指头包扎起来。

一条隧道　a tunnel

We will have to cut a tunnel through thc hill.

我们得开凿一条隧道通过这座山。

一条沟　a ditch

There is a ditch by the side of the road.

路边有一条沟。

一条小溪　a small stream

A small stream runs across it.

一条小溪从这里流过。

一条小船 a boat

By constant endeavour he succeeded in building a boat.

经过不断的努力，他造好了一条小船。

一条标语 a slogan

Above the blackboard there is a slogan.

黑板的上方有一条标语。

一条鱼 a fish

He caught a fish.

他抓到了一条鱼。

一条裙子 a skirt

Mary bought a skirt yesterday.

昨天玛丽买了一条裙子。

一条蛇 a snake

When Mara saw a snake crawling along the path, she screamed.

玛拉看见一条蛇沿着小路爬行时便尖叫了起来。

一条腿 a leg

We didn't know the cheerful athlete was suffering from a seriously injured leg.

我们不知道那位情绪高昂的运动员一条腿受了重伤，正在忍痛坚持。

一条心 of one heart and mind (of one mind)

If we are all of one heart and mind, we can change clay into gold.

众人一条心，黄土变成金。

贴 tiē

仅用于膏药。

一贴……a piece of.

一贴膏药　a piece of medicated plaster
Tom gave me two pieces of medicated plaster.
汤姆给了我两贴膏药。

帖 tiě

用于配合在一起的若干味汤药。

一帖……a dose of.

一帖药　a dose of herbal medicine
I need four doses of herbal medicine.
我要四帖药。

听 tīng

用于听装物品。

一听……a can of; a tin of.

听肉(鱼)　a can (tin) of meat (fish)
There is a can of meat in the refrigerator.
电冰箱里有一听肉。

一听柑橘汁　a can (tin) of orange juice
If you add two cans (tins) of orange juice to the
soup it will taste better.

如果加两听柑橘汁进去，这汤吃起来更有味。

一听饼干　a tin of biscuits

Send round to the grocer's for a tin of biscuits.

通知杂货店送一听饼干来。

挺　tǐng

> 仅用于机关枪。

一挺机关枪　a machine gun

They have over sixty machine guns, both light and heavy.

他们共有六十余挺轻重机关枪。

通　tōng/tòng

> ①用于电报、文书；②用于语言或动作的次数或回数，常置于句末。

一通电报　a telegram

This is a telegram from the company.

这是公司发来的一通电报。

一通文书　a document

Please take this document to the manager's office.

请把这(一)通文书送到经理办公室去。

一通　(give somebody) a talking-to

I'll give him a good talking-to when I meet him.

我见到他时会好好地说他一通。

桶 tǒng

用于桶装物品。

一桶……a barrel of; a bucket of; a drum of; a pail of.

一桶鲱鱼　a barrel of herring
How much shall I pay for a barrel of herring?
买一桶鲱鱼我要付多少钱？

一桶石灰水　a bucket of whitewash
There's a bucket of whitewash in front of the house.
屋子前面有一桶石灰水。

一桶油　a drum of oil
There are only five drums of oil left.
只剩五桶油了。

一桶水　a pail of water
He asked me to fetch a pail of water.
他叫我去打一桶水来。

头 tóu

①用于蒜；②用于牛、骡、驴、猪、羊等家畜。

一头……a bulb of; a head of.

一头蒜　a bulb of garlic
Could I have a bulb of garlic?
给我一头蒜好吗？

一头牛 a cow

His uncle keeps a cow.

他叔父养了一头牛。

团 tuán

> 用于聚集或堆集成团的东西。

一团……a ball of; a cloud of; a mass of; a lump of.

一团毛线 a ball of wool

She put a ball of wool into her handbag and said with a smile: "Do you really love me?"

她把一团毛线放进手提包里，笑着说："你真的爱我吗？"

一团烟雾 a cloud of smoke

A cloud of smoke suddenly appeared above the factory.

工厂上空突然出现一团烟雾。

一团湿面 a lump of dough

Don't dirty this lump of dough.

别把这团湿面弄脏了。

一团热气 a mass of hot air

There came a mass of hot air from the kitchen.

从厨房里吹来一团热气。

丸 wán

> 用于丸药。

一丸药　a pill

The doctor advised me to take two pills three times a day.

医生建议我一次服两丸，一日服三次。

碗　wǎn

用于碗装物品。

一碗……a bowl of.

一碗饭　a bowl of rice

A bowl of rice, please.

请来一碗饭。

一碗汤　a bowl of soup

There is nothing like a bowl of hot soup on a cold winter day.

在寒冷的冬天，有一碗热汤就再好不过了。

汪　wāng

用于成片的液体，与"摊"同义。

一汪……a puddle of; a pool of.

一汪水　a puddle of water (a pool of water)

There is a puddle of water at the street corner.

街道拐角处有一汪水。

尾　wěi

仅用于鱼，与"条"同义。

一尾鱼　a fish

There are two fresh fish in the basket.

篮子里有两尾鲜鱼。

味　wèi

指中药配方，药物中的一种为一味。

一味……ingredient

一味药　One of the ingredients is a medicinal herb

The prescription specifies eight medicinal herbs.

这个方子共八味药。

位　wèi

仅用于人，含敬意。

一位朋友　a friend

A friend came to see you yesterday but you were not in.

昨天，一位朋友来看你，可是你不在家。

一位客人　a guest

I'm going to meet a guest at the station.

我到车站去接一位客人。

一位游泳能手　a good swimmer

You have to practise if you want to be an expert cook, a safe driver, or a good swimmer.

你要想成为一位熟练的厨师，一位安全驾驶员，一位游泳能手，就得反复练习。

一位将军   a general

There is no one to match him as a general.

作为一位将军，他是无与伦比的。

窝 wō

> ①用于一胎所生的或一次所孵出的动物；
> ②用于聚集在一起的人，含贬义。

一窝……a brood of; a litter of.

一窝小鸡   a brood of chickens

Grandma Li keeps a brood of chickens.

李大妈养了一窝小鸡。

一窝小猪   a litter of piglets

A litter of piglets ran in all directions.

一窝小猪四处乱跑。

一窝小猫   a litter of kittens

Hob likes playing with (a litter of) kittens.

霍伯喜欢同(一窝)小猫玩耍。

席 xí

> 用于谈话或酒宴的次数。

一席话   a talk (a conversation)

Having a talk with you for one night is really better than to study for ten years.

与君一席话，胜读十年书。

一席酒(筵)   a banquet (a feast)

系列 xì liè

用于许多有关联的事情、产品、书籍等。

一系列……a series of; a train of.

一系列试验 a series of experiments
Then they began a series of experiments.
然后，他们开始了一系列试验。

一系列问题 a series of problems
In the course of the experiments, they came across a series of problems.
在实验过程中，他们碰到了一系列问题。

一系列著作 a series of works
He produced a series of works in rapid succession.
他接连发表了一系列著作。

一系列措施 a series of measures
We shall take a series of measures to increase production.
我们将采取一系列措施以增加生产。

一系列胜利 a series of victories
They overcame one difficulty after another and won a series of victories.
他们克服了一个又一个困难，赢得了一系列胜利。

一系列主意 a series of ideas
He proposed a series of ideas at the meeting.
他在会上提出了一系列主意。

一系列事件 a train of events (a series of events)
His speech led to a train of events.
他的讲话导致一系列的事件。

一系列不幸　a train of misfortunes (a series of misfortunes)

He is a poor man suffering from a train of misfortunes.

他真是一个可怜的人，有着一系列不幸。

下　xià

用于动作发生的次数，常置句末。

(敲了)一下门　(give) a knock at the door
She gave three knocks at the door.
她敲了三下门。

(打了)一下　(strike) one
The clock has just struck four.
钟刚打过四下。

线　xiàn

用于抽象事物，前面数词仅用"一"。

一线……a beam of; a flash of; a gleam of; a glimmer of; a ray of.

一线光明(光亮)　a gleam of light
A gleam of light came from under the door.
从门下面射出一线光亮来。

一线希望　a glimmer of hope (a ray of hope)
There is still a glimmer of hope.
还有一线希望。

箱 xiāng

用于箱装物品。

一箱······**a case of; a chest of; a crate of; a box of.**

一箱鸡蛋 a case of eggs
We bought a case of eggs and a basket of fish.
我们买了一箱鸡蛋和一筐鱼。

一箱茶叶 a chest of tea
They hid it in a chest of tea.
他们把它藏在一箱茶叶里面。

一箱啤酒 a crate of beer
They drank a whole crate of beer last night.
昨晚他们喝了一整箱啤酒。

一箱苹果 a crate of apples
We'll get a crate of apples for the evening party.
我们将为晚会准备一箱苹果。

一箱书 a box of books
All I have is a box of books.
我的全部财产就是一箱书。

项 xiàng

用于分项目的事物。

一项公报 a communiqué
A joint communiqué was issued on May 5.
五月五日发表了一项联合公报。

一项工程 a project

They let the project drag on indefinitely.

他们无限期地拖延一项工程。

一项行动计划 a plan of action

They plotted out a plan of action.

他们订出了一项行动计划。

一项基金 a fund

They decided to set up a fund for this purpose.

他们决定为此专立一项基金。

一项建议 a suggestion

He came up with a suggestion.

他随便提出了一项建议。

一项协议 an agreement

After much talk they came to an agreement.

费了许多口舌，他们终于达成了一项协议。

一项条款 a clause

We were about to sign the contract when we discovered that the lawyer had tagged on a clause that we could not approve.

我们正要签订合同时，发现律师添上了一项我们不能同意的条款。

一项任务 a task

We were called upon to carry out an urgent task.

我们被指派去执行一项紧急任务。

宿 xiǔ

指整个夜间，一夜为一宿。

一宿 one night

I went to see my aunt and stayed at her home for one night.

我看望过姑妈，并在她家呆了一宿。

巡 xún

指给全座斟酒的次数。

一巡……a round of; a helping of.

一巡酒　a round of wine
The beautiful bride served wine to all the guests.
那位漂亮的新娘给所有的客人斟了一巡酒。
The wine has gone round three times.
酒过三巡。

眼 yǎn

①用于井；②用于视觉器官动作的次数。

一眼井　a well
There is a well in our garden.
我们的庭院中有一眼井。
（瞪了他）一眼　(give him) a hard look
（瞥了他）一眼　(shoot) a glance (at him)

样 yàng

用于事物的种类，与"种"同义。

一样……a kind of; a type of.

一样菜　a kind of vegetable

There were several kinds of vegetables on the table.

桌上有好几样菜。

页　yè

指纸的一张为一页，指书中的一张或一面为一页。

一页……a leaf of; a piece of; a sheet of.

一页　a leaf (a sheet, a page)

Someone has torn a page out of this book.

有人从这本书上撕去一页。

员　yuán

主要用于武将。

一员大将　an able general

His father is an able general.

他的父亲是一员大将。

扎　zā

用于捆起来或束起来的东西。

一扎……a sheaf of; a bundle of.

一扎手稿   a sheaf of manuscripts

He put a sheaf of manuscripts into the drawer and left without saying a word.

他把一扎手稿放进抽屉里，不打招呼就离开了。

一扎文件   (a bundle of papers)

We saw a bundle of papers on his desk.

我们看见他的办公桌上有一扎文件。

一扎信件   a sheaf of letters

遭 zāo

①指事情发生的次数或回数；②指周数。

一遭   the first time

This is the first time I have ever spoken to such a big audience.

在这么多人面前讲话我还是头一遭。

(绕)一遭   (wind) round once

He wound the string round twice.

他用绳子绕两遭。

(走)一遭   (make) a trip

I made a trip to Hong Kong.

我到香港走了一遭。

则 zé

用于分项目或自成段落的文字的条数。

一则……**an item of; a piece of.**

一则新闻(消息)　an item of news (a piece of news)

There's an interesting item of news in the paper today.

今天报上有一则有趣的消息(新闻)。

张　zhāng

用于纸张、票据、床、桌、皮、嘴、弓等。

一张……a piece of; a sheet of; a slip of.

一张纸　a piece of paper (a sheet of paper)

A piece of paper came fluttering out of the window.

一张纸从窗口飘了出来。

一张条子　a slip of paper (a note)

She slipped me a note.

她悄悄地塞给我一张条子。

一张卡片　a card

He pencilled the number on a card and handed it to me.

他用铅笔把号码写在一张卡片上交给了我。

一张地图　a map

I bought a map of the world as well as some picture books.

我买了几本连环画，还买了一张世界地图。

一张明信片　a postcard

She sent me a postcard asking for your address.

她寄给我一张明信片打听你的地址。

一张票　a ticket

Will you get me a ticket?

你能给我弄到一张票吗?

一张支票 a cheque

He immediately sat down and made out a cheque.

他立即坐下来，开了一张支票。

一张收据 a receipt

After he had paid the bill, the cashier made out a receipt for him.

他付款后，那位收款员就开给他一张收据。

一张帐单 a bill

There was a bill along with the parcel.

包裹里附了一张帐单。

一张相 a picture (a photograph)

I want to have my picture taken.

我想照一张相。

一张皮 leather

This bag was made of leather.

这个袋子是用一张皮做成的。

一张桌子 a table (a desk)

The meal was set out on a long table.

饭菜摆在一张长桌上。

一张床 a bed

A table cannot be used as a bed.

一张桌子不能作为一张床来用。

一张嘴 a mouth (tongue)

Miss Li has a sharp tongue.

李小姐有一张严厉的嘴。

阵 zhèn

用于事情或动作经过的段落。

一阵……a bout of; a burst of; a clap of; a fit of; a flurry of; a gale of; a gust of; a hail of; an outburst of; a roar of; a round of; a spasm of; a spate of; a spatter of; a spell of; a squall; a storm of; a torrent of; a volley of; a waft of.

一阵流行性感冒　a bout of influenza

He just got over a bout of influenza.

他刚患过一阵流行性感冒。

一阵炮火　a burst of gunfire

They heard a burst of gunfire.

他们听到了一阵炮火声。

一阵泪水　a torrent of tears

She burst into tears when she heard it.

她听到这消息后，一阵泪水（一股泪水）从她眼中夺眶而出。

一阵雷鸣　a clap of thunder

A sudden clap of thunder woke me.

一阵突然的雷鸣使我惊醒。

一阵大笑　a roar of laughter

Hearing his joke, she went off into a roar of laughter.

听了他的笑话，她突然发出一阵大笑。

一阵兴奋　a flurry of excitement

She got carried away in a flurry of excitement, but we brought her down to earth by reminding her of the tasks waiting to be done.

她在一阵兴奋之中有些想入非非，但是我们提醒她还有许多事要做，才使她从幻想回到现实中来。

一阵大风　a gale

The old tree was blown down in a gale.

那棵老树被一阵风刮倒了。

一阵笑声 an outburst of laughter

This remark brought an outburst of laughter.

这句话引起了一阵笑声。

一阵大怒 paroxysms of anger

Hearing the news, he burst into paroxysms of anger.

听到这消息，他顿时一阵大怒。

一阵风 a gust of wind (a blast of wind)

Scarcely had he opened the door when a gust of wind blew the candle out.

他刚开门，一阵风就把蜡烛吹灭了。

一阵暖风 a warm wind

A warm wind came blowing over the boundless sea.

从无边的海上吹来一阵暖风。

一阵冷风 a cold wind

Towards evening a cold wind sprang up.

傍晚时分，刮起了一阵冷风。

一降微风 a breeze

A breeze suddenly sprang up from the east.

突然从东边吹来了一阵微风。

一阵欢呼声 a roar of cheering

A roar of cheering broke out.

响起了一阵欢呼声。

一阵掌声 a round of of applause

His speech drew round after round of hearty applause.

他的讲话博得一阵又一阵的热烈掌声。

一阵雨 a shower

We were caught in a shower on our way to school.

在去学校的途中，我们遇上了一阵雨。

一阵雷雨 a thunderstorm

We had no sooner set out than a thunderstorm broke.

我们刚出发就碰上了一阵雷雨。

一阵暴雨 a heavy shower (a downpour, a torrent of rain)

As we came up from the bus terminus, a heavy shower caught us.

我们刚从车站走出来，就碰上了一阵暴雨。

一阵疼痛 a spasm of pain

I felt a spasm of pain in my arm.

我感到手臂一阵疼痛。

一阵子弹 a hail of bullets

From the left came a hail of bullets as the enemy opened fire.

敌人开了火，从左边射来了一阵子弹。

一阵头晕 a spell of dizziness

She had a spell of dizziness but soon pulled out of it.

她一阵头晕，可是马上就好了。

一阵香气 a waft of perfume

A waft of perfume greeted us.

一阵香味向我们扑鼻而来。

帧 zhèng

仅用于字画。

一帧油画　an oil painting

He paid a lot of money for an oil painting.

他花了一大笔钱买了一帧油画。

支　zhī

用于笔、烟、队伍、歌曲、灯泡光度等。

一支……a stick of; a contingent of.

一支粉笔　a piece of chalk

Give me a piece of chalk.

给我一支粉笔吧。

一支军队　a contingent of troops

A contingent of troops were besieged in the snow covered mountains.

一支军队被围困在雪山之中。

一支钢笔　a pen

I've picked up a pen, but it doesn't answer to the description you gave.

我拾到了一支钢笔，可是它不象你说的那支笔。

一支烟斗　a pipe

He presented his father with a pipe as a birthday present.

他送给他父亲一支烟斗作为生日的礼品。

一支香烟　a cigarette

He had a cigarette in his mouth.

他嘴里叼着一支香烟。

一支歌　a song

She sang a new song at the party.

她在聚会上唱了一支新歌。

只　zhī

> ①用于飞禽、走兽；②用于某些成对东西中的一个；③用于某些器具。

一只羊　a sheep
A sheep fell into a pit, and I helped it out.
一只羊掉进坑里，我把它救了出来。

一只手镯　a bracelet
Her mother gave her a gold bracelet.
她妈妈给她一只金手镯。

一只老虎　a tiger
They compared me to a tiger.
他们把我比作一只老虎。

一只狼　a wolf
That dog looks like a wolf.
那条狗看上去象一只狼。

一只鸟　a bird
I wish I were a bird.
假如我是一只小鸟就好了。

一只猫　a cat
She was given a cat to keep.
人家给她一只猫喂养。

一只鸭　a duck
There was a splash in the pond, and a duck
bobbed up.
池塘里溅起一阵水花，一只鸭从水里钻了出来。

一只鸡　a chicken
My mother bought a chicken this morning and I
can have chicken broth again.

我母亲今天上午买了一只鸡，我又有鸡汤喝了。

一只兔子　a hare (a rabbit)

The dog is running after a hare.

那条狗正在追捕一只野兔。

一只耳朵　an ear

一只袜子　a sock

一只手提箱　a suitcase

枝 zhī

①用于带枝子的花朵；②用于杆状的东西。

一枝梅花　a spray of plum blossoms (a branch of plum blossoms)

She gave me a spray of plum blossoms.

她送给我一枝梅花。

一枝蜡烛　a candle

There is a candle on his desk.

他的书桌上有一枝蜡烛。

一枝步枪　a rifle

种 zhǒng

用于人和任何事物，表示种类。

一种……a kind of; a sort of.

一种液体　a liquid

Water is a liquid, and the commonest too.

水是一种液体，也是最普通的液体。

一种物质　matter

For a long time air was thought of as not being matter, that is, not having weight and occupying space.

空气长时期曾被认为不是一种物质，也就是说，它没有重量和不占有空间。

一种水果　a fruit

An apple is a fruit.

苹果是一种水果。

一种材料　a kind of material

Steel is an important building material.

钢是一种重要的建筑材料。

一种人　the kind of person

He is the kind of person who would flatter you to your face, and then malign you behind your back.

他是那么一种人，当面奉承，背后诽谤。

一种方法　one way

Heating substances is one way of breaking them down.

给物质加热是使它们分解的一种方法。

一种义务　an obligation

To pay taxes is an obligation.

纳税是一种义务。

一种武器　a weapon

The atom bomb is a weapon of mass slaughter.

原子弹是一种大规模屠杀的武器。

周　zhōu

用于绕圈次数，与"遭"同义。

(绕场)一周 (make) a circuit of the arena
The athletes made a circuit of the arena.
运动员绕场一周。

株 zhū

用于植物，与"棵"同义。

一株玫瑰 a rose
一株松树 a pine

桩 zhuāng

用于事情，与"件"同义。

一桩大事 an important matter
This is an important matter. We must deal with it seriously.
这是一桩大事。我们必须认真对待。
一桩喜事 a happy event
一桩买卖 a business transaction

幢 zhuàng

用于房屋，与"栋"同义。

一幢房子 a house (a building)
David bought a house on a side street.
大卫在一条小街上买了一幢房子。

一幢三层楼房　a three-storey building
They are building a three-storey building.
他们正在建造一幢三层楼的房子。

桌 zhuō

用于桌上放的食物或桌旁坐的人。

一桌……a table of.

一桌饭菜　a meal
They have prepared a meal for us.
他们为我们准备了一桌饭菜。

一桌客人　a table of guests
There are three tables of guests at dinner.
有三桌人进餐。

子 zǐ

用于能用手指招住的一束细长的东西。

一子……a bundle of; a hank of.

一子挂面　a bundle of fine, dried noodles
There is bundle of fine, dried noodles in the
basket.
篮子里有一子挂面。

一子毛线　a hank of wool
She asked me to buy two hanks of wool for her.
她请我给她买两子毛线。

宗 zōng

用于心事、货物等。

一宗心事　a matter that worries one
一(大)宗货物　a large quantity of goods

组 zǔ

用于事物或人的集体。

一组……a group of; a set of.

一组司机　a group of drivers
We are training a group of drivers.
我们正在训练一组司机。

一组学生　a group of students
A group of students often come here to work with us.
一组学生经常到这里来同我们一道工作。

一组邮票　a set of stamps
The post office has issued a set of stamps commemorating the achievements of our country.
邮政局发行了一组邮票，纪念我国建设方面的成就。

尊 zūn

①用于神佛塑像；②用于大炮,与"门"同义。

一尊塑像　a statue

A statue was set up in memory of the great inventor.

为纪念这位伟大的发明家而竖立了一尊塑像。

一尊大炮　a cannon (a piece of artillery)

座 zuò

> 常用于较大或固定的物体或地方。

一座水库　a reservoir

In the three years that followed, they built a reservoir and several small factories.

在以后的三年中，他们修建了一座水库和几家小型工厂。

一座公园　a park

The hill has been laid out as a park.

这座小山布置成了一座公园。

一座桥　a bridge

Follow this road until you get to a bridge.

沿着这条路走，直到你走到一座桥跟前。

一座城市　a city

Singapore is a garden city.

新加坡是一座花园城市。

一座铜像　a bronze statue

一座山　a mountain

一座湖　a lake

As we climbed to the top of the pagoda, we could see a big lake.

我们爬上塔顶时，看到了一座大湖。

英汉索引表

branch	根	gēn	54
	门	mén	89
	枝	zhī	140
breath	丝	sī	111
brood	批	pī	95
	群	qún	104
	窝	wō	125
bucket	担	dàn	26
	桶	tǒng	121
bulb	头	tóu	121
bunch	把	bǎ	1
	班	bān	3
	串	chuàn	20
	簇	cù	23
	束	shù	110
bundle	把	bǎ	1
	包	bāo	6
	捆	kǔn	80
	束	shù	110
	子	zǐ	143
burst	股	gǔ	56
	阵	zhèn	134
cake	块	kuài	76
can	听	tīng	119
caravan	队	duì	41
carton	条	tiáo	116
case	盒	hé	60
	起	qǐ	103
	箱	xiāng	128
cask	桶	tǒng	121
casket	盒	hé	60
category	类	lèi	81
cauldron	锅	guō	59

chain	连串	lián chuàn	83
chest	箱	xiāng	128
chunk	段	duàn	36
	块	kuài	76
circle	群	qún	104
clap	阵	zhèn	134
class	班	bān	3
	届	jiè	69
	期	qī	103
cloak	层	céng	14
cloud	群	qún	104
	团	tuán	122
clump	丛	cóng	22
	簇	cù	23
	蓬	péng	94
cluster	串	chuàn	20
	簇	cù	23
	墩	dūn	44
	群	qún	104
	束	shù	110
coat	层	céng	14
	道	dào	27
coil	卷	juǎn	71
	盘	pán	93
colony	群	qún	104
	窝	wō	125
column	队	duì	41
company	群	qún	104
congregation	群	qún	104
contingent	支	zhī	138
copy	册	cè	13
	份	fèn	48
couple	对	duì	42

group	群	qún	104	jar	缸	gāng	53
	组	zǔ	144		罐	guàn	59
gust	股	gǔ	56	jet	股	gǔ	56
	阵	zhèn	134	jug	罐	guàn	59
hamper	筐	kuāng	79	keg	桶	tǒng	121
	篮	lán	81	kettle	壶	hú	62
hail	阵	zhèn	134	kind	类	lèi	81
handful	把	bǎ	1		样	yàng	130
	撮	cuō	24		种	zhǒng	140
	块	kuài	76	layer	层	céng	14
	捧	pěng	95	leaf	根	gēn	54
hank	束	shù	110		页	yè	131
	子	zǐ	143	leg	段	duàn	36
head	棵	kē	72	length	段	duàn	36
	头	tóu	121		幅	fú	50
heap	叠	dié	33		节	jié	68
	堆	duī	38		截	jié	69
heat	炉	lú	86	line	层	céng	14
helping	份	fèn	48		道	dào	27
	客	kè	73		行	háng	60
herd	群	qún	104		句	jù	70
hive	群	qún	104		排	pái	91
	箱	xiāng	128		趟	tàng	114
horde	股	gǔ	56	list	份	fèn	48
	群	qún	104	litter	窝	wō	125
host	群	qún	104	load	车	chē	18
huddle	堆	duī	38		担	dàn	26
	群	qún	104	loaf	块	kuài	76
ingot	锭	dìng	35		条	tiáo	116
ingredient	味	wèi	124	lock	绺	liǔ	85
issue	期	qī	103	lot	番	fān	46
item	条	tiáo	116	lump	笔	bǐ	10
	则	zé	132		块	kuài	76

lump	团	tuán	122		pair	双	shuāng	110
mantle	层	céng	14			条	tiáo	116
mass	堆	duī	38		pan	锅	guō	60
	片	piàn	99		party	批	pī	95
	团	tuán	122			群	qún	104
meal	顿	dùn	44		patch	丛	cóng	22
mob	伙	huǒ	63		period	段	duàn	36
	群	qún	104			期	qī	103
morsel	点	diǎn	30			堂	táng	114
	口	kǒu	75		petal	班	bàn	3
mouthful	口	kǒu	75			片	piàn	99
mug	杯	bēi	7		phase	期	qī	103
mountain	堆	duī	38		piece	点	diǎn	30
multitude	群	qún	104			段	duàn	36
muster	批	pī	95			番	fān	46
nest	套	tào	115			方	fāng	46
nip	口	kǒu	75			份	fèn	48
number	批	pī	95			幅	fú	50
ounce	点	diǎn	30			个	gè	53
outburst	阵	zhèn	134			根	gēn	54
pack	包	bāo	6			件	jiàn	67
	副	fù	52			块	kuài	76
	伙	huǒ	64			门	mén	89
	派	pài	92			篇	piān	98
	群	qún	104			条	tiáo	116
	套	tào	115			贴	tiē	119
	箱	xiāng	128			页	yè	131
package	包	bāo	6			则	zé	132
packet	包	bāo	6			张	zhāng	133
pail	桶	tǒng	121		pile	叠	dié	33
pair	把	bǎ	1			堆	duī	38
	对	duì	42		pinch	撮	cuō	24
	副	fù	51		plate	碟	dié	34